A Treatise Concerning
THE PRINCIPLES OF
HUMAN KNOWLEDGE

George Berkeley

Edited and with a Preface by
Thomas J. McCormack

D1113426

Dover Publications, Inc.
Mineola, New York

DOVER PHILOSOPHICAL CLASSICS

Bibliographical Note

This Dover edition, first published in 2003, is an unabridged reprint of the edition published by The Open Court Publishing Company, La Salle, Il., 1940. *A Treatise Concerning the Principles of Human Knowledge* was first published in Dublin in 1710.

Library of Congress Cataloging-in-Publication Data

Berkeley, George, 1685–1753.
  A treatise concerning the principles of human knowledge / George Berkeley ; edited and with a preface by Thomas J. McCormack.
      p. cm. — (Dover philosophical classics)
    ISBN 0-486-43253-X (pbk.)
    1. Knowledge, Theory of. I. McCormack, Thomas J. II. Title. III. Series.

B1331.M33 2003
121—dc22

                                                    2003057277

Manufactured in the United States of America
Dover Publications, Inc., 31 East 2nd Street, Mineola, N.Y. 11501

EDITOR'S PREFACE.

BERKELEY'S *Treatise Concerning the Principles of Human Knowledge*, of which a reprint is here produced as the fourth of the series of Philosophical Classics of the Religion of Science Library, was first published in Dublin in 1710. The second edition, the last of the author's life-time, appeared in London in 1734, in the same volume with the third edition of the *Three Dialogues Between Hylas and Philonous*, a reprint of which has also been issued in this series as a companion-piece to the *Principles*. The text of both reprints embodies all the essential matter of the editions of Berkeley's life-time.

The *Principles*, published when the author was only twenty-six, is the most systematic of all of Berkeley's expositions of his theory of knowledge: it was the direct outgrowth of the *Essay Towards a New Theory of Vision* (1709), which sought to banish the metaphysical abstractions of Absolute Space and Extension from philosophy, and was itself mainly concerned with the abolition of Abstract Matter and of the ontological and theological corollaries of that concept. The *Dialogues* treat of substantially the same subjects, but are more familiar and elegant in form and are devoted in the main to the refutation of the most plausible popular and philosophical objections to the new doctrine. The two books mark a distinctively new epoch in philosophy and science, and together afford a comprehensive survey of Berkeley's doctrines, placing within the reach of every reader in remarkably brief compass opinions which have profoundly influenced the course of intellectual history. Works of this kind have been almost invariably distinguished by their brevity. "I had no inclination," is Berkeley's characteristic remark, "to trouble the world with large volumes. What I have done was rather with the view of giving hints to thinking men, who have leisure and curiosity to go to the bottom of things, and pursue them in their own minds, Two or three times reading these small tracts, and making what is read the occasion of thinking, would, I believe, render the whole familiar and easy to the mind, and take off that shocking appearance which hath often been observed to attend speculative truths."

Berkeley's philosophy having been the victim of much popular, and even professional, misapprehension, it shall be our endeavor in these prefatory remarks to give by appropriate quotations and digests a synthesis of current philosophical opinion concerning his doctrines, to point out his relation to his predecessors, to indicate certain peculiarities of terminology and thought necessary to the understanding of his theory, and to show finally wherein certain of his analyses have been rendered antiquated by modern scientific inquiry. We shall begin by reproducing the sketch of his life and aims given in Lewes's *Biographical History of Philosophy* (1845), a work which, though on technical points partisan and not always trustworthy, has at least the merit of a vivacious style.

LIFE OF BERKELEY.

"There are few men of whom England has better reason to be proud than of George Berkeley, Bishop of Cloyne; for to extraordinary merits as a thinker and writer he united the most exquisite purity and generosity of character; and it is still a moot point whether he was greater in head or heart.

"He was born on the 12th of March, 1685, at Kilcrin, in the county of Kilkenny, Ireland. He was educated at Trinity College, Dublin, and was in 1707 admitted as a fellow. In 1709 he published his *Essay Towards a New Theory of Vision*, which made an epoch in science ;* and the year after, his *Principles of Human Knowledge*, which made an epoch in metaphysics. After this he came to London, where he was received with open arms. Ancient learning, exact science, polished society, modern literature, and the fine arts, contributed to adorn and enrich the mind

---

*This statement is hardly exact. The *Essay Towards a New Theory of Vision* was a psychological rather than a scientific treatise. The work has been well characterised by Prof. A. C. Fraser in his edition of the collected works of Berkeley, Vol. I., page 5, as follows: "The treatise is a professed account of the facts, the whole facts, and nothing but the facts of which we are visually conscious, as distinguished from pretended facts and metaphysical abstractions, which confused thought, an irregular exercise of imagination, or an abuse of words had substituted for them. It is a contribution to the psychological analysis of the fact of vision, and not a deduction from merely physical experiments in optics or the physiology of the eye."—*Editor.*

of this accomplished man. All his contemporaries agreed with the Satirist in ascribing

> To Berkeley every virtue under heaven.

Adverse factions and hostile wits concurred only in loving, admiring, and contributing to advance him. The severe sense of Swift endured his visions; the modest Addison endeavored to reconcile Clarke to his ambitious speculations. His character converted the satire of Pope into fervid praise. Even the discerning, fastidious, and turbulent Atterbury said, after an interview with him, "so much learning, so much knowledge, so much innocence, and such humility, I did not think had been the portion of any but angels, till I saw this gentleman." '*

"His acquaintance with the wits led to his contributing to the *Guardian.* He became chaplain and afterwards secretary to the Earl of Peterborough, whom he accompanied on his embassy to Sicily. He subsequently made the tour of Europe with Mr. Ashe; and at Paris met Malebranche, with whom he had an animated discussion on the ideal theory. In 1724 he was made dean of Derry. This was worth eleven hundred pounds a year to him; but he resigned it in order to dedicate his life to the conversion of the North American savages, stipulating only with the Government for a salary of one hundred pounds a year. On this romantic and generous expedition he was accompanied by his young wife. He set sail for Rhode Island, carrying with him a valuable library of books and the bulk of his property. But, to the shame of the Government, be it said, the promises made him were not fulfilled, and after seven years of single-handed endeavour he was forced to return to England, having spent the greater part of his fortune in vain.

"He was made Bishop of Cloyne in 1734. When he wished to resign, the King would not permit him; and being keenly alive to the evils of non-residence, he made an arrangement before leaving Cloyne whereby he settled 200*l.* a year during his absence on the poor. In 1752 he removed to Oxford, where, on the evening of the 14th January, in 1753, he was suddenly seized, while reading, with palsy of the heart, and died almost instantaneously.

"Of his numerous writings we cannot here speak; two only belong to our subject: the *Principles of Knowledge*, and the *Dialogues of Hylas and Philonous.* [His other most important

---

* Sir James Mackintosh.

philosophical work was *Alciphron, or the Minute Philosopher* (1733)]. We hope to remove some of the errors and prejudices with which his name is encrusted. We hope to show that, even in what are called his wildest moods, Berkeley was a plain, sincere, deep-thinking man, not a sophist playing with paradoxes to display his skill.

THE TRADITIONAL MISCONCEPTION OF BERKELEY'S IDEALISM.

"All the world has heard of Berkeley's Idealism, and innumerable 'coxcombs' have vanquished it 'with a grin.'* Ridicule has not been sparing of it. Argument has not been wanting. It has been laughed at, written at, talked at, shrieked at. That it has been *understood* is not so apparent. Few writers seem to have honestly read and appreciated his works; and those few are certainly not among his antagonists.† In reading the criticisms upon his theory it is quite ludicrous to notice the constant iteration of trivial objections which, trivial as they are, Berkeley had often anticipated. In fact, the critics misunderstood him, and then reproached him for his inconsistency—inconsistency, not with *his* principles, but with *theirs*. They force a meaning upon his words which he had expressly rejected; and then triumph over him because he did not pursue their principles to the extravagances which would have resulted from them.

"When Berkeley denied the existence of matter, he simply denied the existence of that unknown *substratum*, the existence of which Locke had declared to be a necessary *inference* from our knowledge of qualities, but the nature of which must ever be altogether hidden from us. Philosophers had assumed the existence of substance, i. e., of a *noumenon* lying underneath all *phenomena* —a substratum supporting all qualities—a *something* in which all accidents *inhere*. This unknown substance Berkeley denies. It is a mere abstraction, he says. If it is unknown, unknowable, it

---

* "And coxcombs vanquish Berkeley with a grin."—*Pope.*

† These words were written in 1845–1846. Since then Prof. A. Campbell Fraser's magnificent edition of Berkeley's collected works (4 vols. Clarendon Press. 1871) and his exhaustive dissertations on Berkeley's doctrines, together with the many excellent histories of philosophy of the last half century, have rendered such misunderstanding, at least on the part of the philosophical public, almost impossible.—*Editor.*

is a figment. and I will none of it; for it is a figment worse than useless; it is pernicious, as the basis of all Atheism. If by matter you understand *that* which is seen, felt, tasted, and touched, then I say matter exists: I am as firm a believer in its existence as any one can be, and *herein I agree with the vulgar*. If, on the contrary, you understand by matter that occult *substratum* which is *not* seen, *not* felt, *not* tasted, and *not* touched—that of which the senses do not, cannot, inform you—then I say I believe not in the existence of matter, and *herein I differ with the philosophers and agree with the vulgar*.

" 'I am not changing things into ideas,' he says, 'but rather ideas into things; since those *immediate objects of perception*, which according to you (Berkeley might have said, according to philosophers) are only *appearances of things*, I take to be the real things themselves.

" '*Hylas:* Things! you may pretend what you please; but it is certain you leave us nothing but the empty forms of things, the *outside of which only strikes the senses*.

" '*Philonous:* What *you* call the empty forms and outside of things seem to *me* the very things themselves. . . . We both therefore agree in this, that we perceive only sensible forms; but herein we differ: you will have them to be empty appearances; I, real beings. In short, *you do not trust your senses; I do*.'

"Berkeley is always accused of having propounded a theory which contradicts the evidence of the senses. That a man who should thus disregard the senses must be out of his, was a ready answer; ridicule was not slow in retort: declamation gave itself elbow-room, and exhibited itself in a triumphant attitude. It was easy to declare (Reid, *Inquiry*) that 'the man who seriously entertains this belief, though in other respects he may be a very good man, as a man may be who believes he is made of glass; yet surely he hath a soft place in his understanding, and hath been hurt by much thinking.'

"Unfortunately for the critics, Berkeley did *not* contradict the evidence of the senses; did *not* propound a theory at variance in this point with the ordinary belief of mankind. His peculiarity is, that he confined himself exclusively to the evidence of the senses. What the senses informed him of, that, and *that only*, would he accept. He held fast to the facts of consciousness; he placed himself resolutely in the centre of the instinctive belief of

mankind : there he took up his stand, leaving to philosophers the
region of supposition, inference, and of occult substances.

"The reproach made to him is really the reproach he made
to philosophers, viz., that they would not trust to the evidence of
their senses; that over and above what the senses told them, they
imagined an occult something of which the senses gave no indica-
tion. 'Now it was against this metaphysical phantom of the brain,'
says an acute critic (*Blackwood's Magazine*, June, 1842, p. 814)
'this crochet-work of philosophers, and against it alone, that all
the attacks of Berkeley were directed. The doctrine that the realities of things were not made for man, and that he must rest satisfied with mere appearances was regarded, and rightly, by him as
the parent of scepticism with all her desolating train. He saw
that philosophy, in giving up the reality immediately within her
grasp, in favor of a reality supposed to be less delusive, which lay
beyond the limits of experience, resembled the dog in the fable,
who, carrying a piece of meat across a river, let the substance slip
from his jaws, while with foolish greed he snatched at the shadow
in the stream. The dog lost his dinner, and philosophy let go her
secure hold upon truth. He therefore sided with the vulgar, who
recognise no distinction between the reality and the appearance of
objects, and repudiating the baseless hypothesis of a world existing unknown and unperceived, he resolutely maintained that what
are called the sensible shows of things are in truth the very things
themselves.'

"True it is that owing to the ambiguities of language Berkeley's theory does not seem to run counter to the ordinary belief of
mankind, because by Matter men commonly understand the seen,
the tasted, the touched, &c.; therefore when the existence of Matter is denied, people naturally suppose that the existence of the
seen, the tasted, and the touched is denied, never suspecting that
Matter, in its philosophical sense, is *not* seen, *not* tasted, *not*
touched. Berkeley has not, it must be confessed, sufficiently
guarded against all ambiguity. Thus he says in one of the opening sections of his *Principles of Human Knowledge*, that "It is
indeed *an opinion strangely prevailing amongst men* that
houses, mountains, rivers, and, in a word, all sensible objects
have an existence, natural or real, distinct from their being perceived by the understanding.' This is striking the key-note false.
It rouses the reader to oppose a coming paradox.

"Yet Berkeley foresaw and answered the objections which Wimpey, Beattie, Reid, and others brought forward. He was not giving utterance to a caprice; he was not spinning an ingenious theory, knowing all the while that it was no more than an ingenuity. He was an earnest thinker, patient in the search after truth. Anxious, therefore, that his speculations should not be regarded as mere dialectical displays, he endeavoured on various occasions to guard himself from misapprehension.

" 'I do not argue against the existence of any one thing that we can apprehend either by sensation or reflection. That the things I see with my eyes and touch with my hands do exist, really exist, I make not the least question. The only thing whose existence I deny is that which philosophers call Matter, or corporeal substance. And in doing this there is no damage done to the rest of mankind, who, I dare say, will never miss it. . . .

" 'If any man thinks we detract from the reality of existence of things, he is very far from understanding what has been premised in the plainest terms I could think of. . . . It will be urged that thus much at least is true, viz., that we take away all corporeal substances. To this my answer is, that if the word *substance* be taken in the vulgar sense for a combination of sensible qualities, such as extension, solidity, weight, &c., this we cannot be accused of taking away.* But if it be taken in the philosophic sense, for the support of accidents or qualities without the mind; then, indeed, I acknowledge that we take it away, if one may be said to take away that which never had any existence, not even in the imagination.

" 'But say what we can, some one perhaps may be apt to reply, he will still believe his senses, and never suffer any arguments, however plausible, to prevail over the certainty of them. Be it so; assert the evidence of sense as high as you please, *we are willing to do the same.* That what I see, hear, and feel, doth exist, i. e., is perceived by me, I no more doubt than I do of my own being; but I do not see how the testimony of sense can be alleged as a proof of anything which is not perceived by sense.' †

"After reading these passages (and more of a similar cast might be quoted) in what terms shall we speak of the trash written

---

*An answer to Dr. Johnson's peremptory refutation of Berkeley, viz., kicking a stone: as if Berkeley ever denied that what we call stones existed!

† *Principles of Human Knowledge*, Sections 35, 36, 37, 40.

to refute Idealism? Where was the acuteness of the Reids and Beatties, when they tauntingly asked why Berkeley did not run his head against a post, did not walk over precipices, &c., as, in accordance with his theory, no pain, no broken limbs, could result?* Where was philosophical acumen, when a tribe of writers could imagine they refuted Berkeley by an appeal to common sense—when they contrasted the instinctive beliefs of mankind with the speculative paradoxes of a philosopher, who expressly took his stand with common sense against philosophers?

"Men trained in metaphysical speculations may find it difficult to conceive the non-existence of an invisible, unknowable substratum; but that the bulk of mankind find it almost impossible to conceive any such substratum is a fact which the slightest inquiry will verify. We have experienced this more than once. We remember a discussion which lasted an entire evening, in which by no power of illustration, by no force of argument, could the idea of this substance, apart from its sensible qualities, be rendered conceivable.

"Berkeley, therefore, in denying the existence of matter, sided with common sense. He thought with the vulgar, that matter was that of which his senses informed him; not an occult something of which he could have no information. The table he saw before him certainly existed: it was hard, polished, coloured, of a certain figure, and cost some guineas. But there was no *phantom table* lying underneath the *apparent table*—there was no invisible substance supporting that table. What he perceived was a table, and nothing more; what he perceived it to be, he would believe it to be, and nothing more. His starting-point was thus what the plain dictates of his senses and the senses of all men furnished."

BERKELEY'S PLACE IN THE HISTORY OF PHILOSOPHY.

"In the philosophies of Descartes (1596–1650) and Locke (1632 –1704)," says Professor R. Adamson in the *Encyclopædia Britan-*

---

* "But what is the consequence? I resolve not to believe my senses. I break my head against a post that comes in my way; I step into a dirty kennel; and after twenty such wise and rational actions I am taken up and clapt into a madhouse. Now I confess I had rather make one of those credulous fools whom nature imposes upon, than of those wise and rational philosophers who resolve to withhold assent at all this expense."—Reid's *Inquiry*, ch. vi., sec. 20. This one passage is as good as a hundred.

nica, "a large share of attention had been directed to the idea of matter, which was held to be the abstract, unperceived background of real experience, and was supposed to give rise to our ideas of external things through its action on the sentient mind. Knowledge, being limited to the ideas produced, could never extend to the unperceived matter, or substance, or cause which produced them, and it became a problem for speculative science to determine the grounds for the very belief in its existence. Philosophy seemed about to end in scepticism or in materialism. Now Berkeley put this whole problem in a new light by pointing out that a preliminary question must be raised and answered. Before we deduce results from such abstract ideas as cause, substance, matter, we must ask what in reality do these mean,—what is the actual content of consciousness which corresponds to these words? Do not all these ideas, when held to represent something which exists absolutely apart from all knowledge of it, involve a contradiction? Are they not truly, when so regarded, inconceivable, and mere arbitrary figments which cannot possibly be realised in consciousness? In putting this question, not less than in answering it, consists Berkeley's distinct originality as a philosopher."

This is what Professor Fraser (*Life and Letters of Berkeley,* p. 364) has termed the "New Question" about space and the material world, for which Berkeley tried in vain to get a hearing his whole life long. With it, according to the same author, he inaugurated a "new and second era in the intellectual revolution which Descartes set agoing. This Second Period in Modern Philosophy has been marked by the sceptical phenomenalism of Hume (now represented by Positivism); the Scotch psychology of Common Sense; and the German critical and dialectical philosophy of Reason."

Berkeley's relations to Leibnitz (1646–1716) and Malebranche (1638–1715) were also characteristic. Knowing the agreement existing between Locke and Spinoza, the champions of systems so remote as empiricism and rationalism, it is not surprising, remarks Dr. A. Weber in his excellent *History of Philosophy,** "to see a disciple of the English philosopher [Berkeley] offering the hand of friendship to Leibnitz and Malebranche, the champions of intellectualism and innate ideas across the sea. Although Locke and his opponents differ on several essential points, they reach practi-

---

*Translated by Professor Thilly, New York, Scribner's, 1896.

cally the same conclusions concerning the world of sense. Male-branche and Leibniz spiritualise matter; they explain it as a confused idea, and ultimately assume a principle endowed with desire and perception, that is, mind. Locke's criticism, on the other hand, does not wholly reject the material world; one half of it is retained. Extension, form, and motion exist outside of us; but neither colors, nor sounds, nor tastes, nor smells exist independently of our sensations. Moreover, Locke attacks the traditional notion of substance, or substratum, and defines real substance as a combination of qualities. Indeed, he goes so far as to say that the idea of corporeal substance or matter is as remote from our conceptions and apprehensions as that of spiritual substance or spirit! Hence, all that was needed to arrive at the negation of matter or absolute spiritualism was to efface the distinction which he had drawn between primary and secondary qualities, and to call all sensible qualities without exception, secondary. This George Berkeley did."

The student should now carefully re-read in this connexion sections 5, 6, 8, 22, 23, 28–36, 50, 86–94 of the *Principles*, where Berkeley's position as to the meaning of reality is defined in unmistakable terms. The subjectivisation of reality, which seems absolute at the start, may be seen gradually to develop in these sections into a species of spiritualistic objectification. Sections 25–27 on causality are important here as showing "that voluntary mental activity is the only Causation in the universe,—that all Power, as well as all Substance, is essentially mental." Berkeley's system is, in fact, an *absolute, monistic spiritualism*, in which the dualism of substances has been completely overcome. "The universe in which we find ourselves is a universe that consists, in the last analysis, of *mind conscious of ideas or phenomena.* The ideas of *sense* appear in an order which, because independent of our individual will, may be called *external* to each of us; and which, being uniform, is capable of being interpreted." (Fraser, I., 121.) Berkeley's theory must be sharply distinguished from Fichte's *subjective* idealism. Objectivity has not suffered in Berkeley's theory; it has simply *been displaced from the realm of unknowable matter to that of knowable mind.* This is a most important feature of Berkeley's philosophy and one that has been nearly always unrecognised.

It is to be remembered in this connexion that Berkeley's sys-

tem is primarily directed against scepticism and irreligion, and
that it has therefore peculiarly merited from both a religious and
philosophical point of view Professor Fraser's epithet of "Theological or Universalised Sensationalism." Berkeley's argument
and position on this point and his relationship to Malebranche (as
to existence and vision in God) come out very clearly in the following quotation from the Second Dialogue Between Hylas and Philonous:

"*Philonous.* I deny that I agreed with you in those notions
that led to Scepticism. You indeed said the *reality* of sensible
things consisted in an *absolute existence* out of the minds of spirits, or distinct from their being perceived. And, pursuant to this
notion of reality, you are obliged to deny sensible things any real
existence: that is, according to your own definition, you profess
yourself a sceptic. But I neither said nor thought the reality of
sensible things was to be defined after that manner. To me it is
evident, for the reasons you allow of, that sensible things cannot
exist otherwise than in a mind or spirit. Whence I conclude, not
that they have no real existence, but that, seeing they depend not
on my thought, and have an existence distinct from being perceived by me, *there must be some other mind wherein they exist*.
As sure, therefore, as the sensible world really exists, so sure is
there an infinite omnipresent Spirit, who contains and supports it.

"*Hylas.* What! this is no more than I and all Christians
hold; nay, and all others too who believe there is a God, and that
He knows and comprehends all things.

"*Phil.* Aye, but here lies the difference. Men commonly believe that all things are known or perceived by God, because they
believe the being of a God; whereas I, on the other side, immediately and necessarily conclude the being of a God, because all
sensible things must be perceived by him.

"*Hyl.* But so long as we all believe the same thing, what matter is it how we come by that belief?

"*Phil.* But neither do we agree in the same opinion. For
philosophers, though they acknowledge all corporeal beings to be
perceived by God, yet they attribute to them an absolute subsistence distinct from their being perceived by any mind whatever,
which I do not. Besides, is there no difference between saying,
There is a God, therefore He perceives all things; and saying,
Sensible things do not really exist; and, if they really exist, they

are necessarily perceived by an infinite mind : therefore there is
an infinite mind, or God? This furnishes you with a direct and
immediate demonstration, from a most evident principle, of the
being of a God. Divines and philosophers had proved beyond all
controversy, from the beauty and usefulness of the several parts
of the creation, that it was the workmanship of God. But that—
setting aside all help of astronomy and natural philosophy, all
contemplation of the contrivance, order, and adjustment of things
—an infinite mind should be necessarily inferred from the bare
existence of the sensible world, is an advantage to them only who
have made this easy reflexion, that the sensible world is that which
we perceive by our several senses; and that nothing is perceived
by the senses beside ideas; and that no idea or an archetype of an
idea can exist otherwise than in a mind. You may now, without
any laborious search into the sciences, without any subtlety of
reason, or tedious length of discourse, oppose and baffle the most
strenuous advocate for Atheism; those miserable refuges, whether
in an eternal succession of unthinking causes and effects, or in a
fortuitous concourse of atoms; those wild imaginations of Vanini,
Hobbes, and Spinoza : in a word, the whole system of Atheism, is
it not entirely overthrown, by this single reflexion on the repugnancy included in supposing the whole, or any part, even the most
rude and shapeless, of the visible world, to exist without mind?"

As to the function and nature of abstraction in thought, and
the reification of general ideas (see the Introduction), Berkeley s
analysis has become classical. Further, he distinctly anticipated,
in his criticism of the metaphysical dogma of the thing-in-itself as
existing independently of the phenomenon, the erroneous and
sceptical conclusions to which the great Kant was afterwards so
strangely led in his *Critique of the Pure Reason*; and in his ani-
madversions on the notions of absolute space, time, etc., upheld
by Newton (sections 110–117), he has in part adumbrated the
strictures of modern scientists.* In his reflexions on mathematics
(sections 118 et seq.) he has not been so fortunate. The difficulties
he saw in the fundamental conceptions of the Infinitesimal Analysis have since been cleared up, and much that he says on this subject has now historical significance only; while as for his conception of the nature of the ego and spiritual substance (sections 137

---

* See Mach, *Mechanics* (Chicago, 1893), pp. 226 et seq., 512.

et seq.), these have been rendered altogether nugatory by modern psychology.[1]

MEANING OF THE WORD "IDEA" IN BERKELEY'S SYSTEM.

A knowledge of Berkeley's peculiar use of the word "idea" is necessary to a perfect understanding of his philosophy, and we may therefore appropriately conclude with a quotation explaining it. "The little word idea," says Professor Fraser in his *Life and Letters of Berkeley* "(and it may be added the so far synonymous terms *sensation* and *phenomenon*—for Berkeley may be called a Sensationalist, or a Phenomenalist, as well as an Idealist) has been a formidable obstruction to the intelligibility of this philosopher. With him it means both *percept* and *image*—not pure *notion* of the understanding. And it is with ideas as actual sensation-perceptions that we have to do exclusively, when we are told by him that the sensible world is composed of *ideas*. Simply to recollect what he means by idea is almost to realise his conception of the universe. When ordinary people are told that *idea* is the stuff or matter of which, according to Berkeley, the real things of the sensible world are composed, they are apt to take this for an assertion that what we call seeing and touching is only fancying; and that what is seen and touched is to be regarded as a mere subjective or private dream of the person's own mind who has the ideas—that it can have no extension or solidity or permanence. Now, Berkeley's ideas include hard and extended *facts*, and are not mere *fancies* of which we are conscious. He calls them ideas because he sees it to be self-evident that facts cannot exist positively without a mind to be percipient of them. Nor are we, on the other hand, to think of Berkeley's ideas, or phenomena perceived in sense, as independent entities which circulate among finite spirits; their actual or intelligible existence consists in being the matter of the experience of a conscious mind—a *sui generis* sort of dependent existence. But no doubt his language is vacillating."

THOMAS J. McCORMACK.

LA SALLE, ILL.

---

* See Ribot's summaries, *Diseases of Personality*, etc., and the discussions in Dr. Paul Carus's *Whence and Whither*, *The Soul of Man*, and the *Primer of Philosophy* (all published by the Open Court Pub. Co., Chicago).

A
TREATISE
Concerning the
PRINCIPLES
OF
Human Knowlege.

PART I.

Wherein the chief Caufes of Error and Difficulty in the *Sciences*, with the Grounds
of *Scepticifm*, *Atheifm*, and *Irreligion*, are
inquir'd into.

By *George Berkeley*, M.A. Fellow of
Trinity-College, Dublin.

DVBLIN:
Printed by AARON RHAMES, for JEREMY
PEPYAT, Bookfeller in *Skinner-Row*, 1710.

TO THE RIGHT HONOURABLE*

THOMAS, EARL OF PEMBROKE, &c.,

KNIGHT OF THE MOST NOBLE ORDER OF THE GARTER, AND ONE OF THE LORDS OF HER MAJESTY'S MOST HONOURABLE PRIVY COUNCIL.

My Lord,

You will perhaps wonder that an obscure person, who has not the honour to be known to your lordship, should presume to address you in this manner. But that a man who has written something with a design to promote Useful Knowledge and Religion in the world should make choice of your lordship for his patron, will not be thought strange by any one that is not altogether unacquainted with the present state of the church and learning, and consequently ignorant how great an ornament and support you are to both. Yet, nothing could have induced me to make you this present of my poor endeavours, were I not encouraged by that candour and native goodness which is so bright a part in your lordship's character. I might add, my lord, that the extraordinary favour and bounty you have been pleased to show towards our Society gave me hopes you would not be unwilling to countenance the studies of one of its members. These considerations determined me to lay this treatise at your lord-

---

*This dedication was not published in the second edition (1734).

ship's feet, and the rather because I was ambitious to have it known that I am with the truest and most profound respect, on account of that learning and virtue which the world so justly admires in your lordship,

My Lord,

Your lordship's most humble
and most devoted servant,
GEORGE BERKELEY.

PREFACE.*

What I here make public has, after a long and scrupulous inquiry, seemed to me evidently true and not unuseful to be known—particularly to those who are tainted with Scepticism, or want a demonstration of the existence and immateriality of God, or the natural immortality of the soul. Whether it be so or no I am content the reader should impartially examine; since I do not think myself any farther concerned for the success of what I have written than as it is agreeable to truth. But, to the end this may not suffer, I make it my request that the reader suspend his judgment till he has once at least read the whole through with that degree of attention and thought which the subject-matter shall seem to deserve. For, as there are some passages that, taken by themselves, are very liable (nor could it be remedied) to gross misinterpretation, and to be charged with most absurd consequences, which, nevertheless, upon an entire perusal will appear not to follow from them; so likewise, though the whole should be read over, yet, if this be done transiently, it is very probable my sense may be mistaken; but to a thinking reader, I flatter myself it will be throughout clear and obvious. As for the characters of novelty and singularity which some of

*This preface was not published in the edition of 1734.

3

the following notions may seem to bear, it is, I hope, needless to make any apology on that account. He must surely be either very weak, or very little acquainted with the sciences, who shall reject a truth that is capable of demonstration, for no other reason but because it is newly known, and contrary to the prejudices of mankind. Thus much I thought fit to premise, in order to prevent, if possible, the hasty censures of a sort of men who are too apt to condemn an opinion before they rightly comprehend it.

INTRODUCTION.

I.

Philosophy being nothing else but the study of wisdom and truth, it may with reason be expected that those who have spent most time and pains in it should enjoy a greater calm and serenity of mind, a greater clearness and evidence of knowledge, and be less disturbed with doubts and difficulties than other men. Yet so it is, we see the illiterate bulk of mankind that walk the high-road of plain common sense, and are governed by the dictates of nature, for the most part easy and undisturbed. To them nothing that is familiar appears unaccountable or difficult to comprehend. They complain not of any want of evidence in their senses, and are out of all danger of becoming Sceptics. But no sooner do we depart from sense and instinct to follow the light of a superior principle, to reason, meditate, and reflect on the nature of things, but a thousand scruples spring up in our minds concerning those things which before we seemed fully to comprehend. Prejudices and errors of sense do from all parts discover themselves to our view; and, endeavouring to correct these by reason, we are insensibly drawn into uncouth paradoxes, difficulties, and inconsistencies, which multiply and grow upon us as we advance in speculation, till at length, having wandered through many intricate mazes, we find ourselves just where we were, or, which is worse, sit down in a forlorn Scepticism.

2. The cause of this is thought to be the obscurity of things, or the natural weakness and imperfection of our understandings. It is said, the faculties we have are few, and those designed by nature for the support and comfort of life, and not to penetrate into the inward essence and constitution of things. Besides, the mind of man being finite, when it treats of things which partake of infinity, it is not to be wondered at if it run into absurdities and contradictions, out of which it is impossible it should ever extricate itself, it being of the nature of infinite not to be comprehended by that which is finite.

3. But, perhaps, we may be too partial to ourselves in placing the fault originally in our faculties, and not rather in the wrong use we make of them. It is a hard thing to suppose that right deductions from true principles should ever end in consequences which cannot be maintained or made consistent. We should believe that God has dealt more bountifully with the sons of men than to give them a strong desire for that knowledge which he had placed quite out of their reach. This were not agreeable to the wonted indulgent methods of Providence, which, whatever appetites it may have implanted in the creatures, doth usually furnish them with such means as, if rightly made use of, will not fail to satisfy them. Upon the whole, I am inclined to think that the far greater part, if not all, of those difficulties which have hitherto amused philosophers, and blocked up the way to knowledge, are entirely owing to ourselves—that we have first raised a dust and then complain we cannot see.

4. My purpose therefore is, to try if I can discover

what those Principles are which have introduced all that doubtfulness and uncertainty, those absurdities and contradictions, into the several sects of philosophy; insomuch that the wisest men have thought our ignorance incurable, conceiving it to arise from the natural dulness and limitation of our faculties. And surely it is a work well deserving our pains to make a strict inquiry concerning the First Principles of Human Knowledge, to sift and examine them on all sides, especially since there may be some grounds to suspect that those lets and difficulties, which stay and embarrass the mind in its search after truth, do not spring from any darkness and intricacy in the objects, or natural defect in the understanding, so much as from false Principles which have been insisted on, and might have been avoided.

5. How difficult and discouraging soever this attempt may seem, when I consider how many great and extraordinary men have gone before me in the like designs, yet I am not without some hopes—upon the consideration that the largest views are not always the clearest, and that he who is short-sighted will be obliged to draw the object nearer, and may, perhaps, by a close and narrow survey, discern that which had escaped far better eyes.

6. In order to prepare the mind of the reader for the easier conceiving what follows, it is proper to premise somewhat, by way of Introduction, concerning the nature and abuse of Language. But the unravelling this matter leads me in some measure to anticipate my design, by taking notice of what seems to have had a chief part in rendering speculation intricate and perplexed, and to have occasioned innumerable errors and difficulties in almost all parts of knowledge. And that

is the opinion that the mind hath a power of framing *abstract ideas* or notions of things. He who is not a perfect stranger to the writings and disputes of philosophers must needs acknowledge that no small part of them are spent about abstract ideas. These are in a more especial manner thought to be the object of those sciences which go by the name of Logic and Metaphysics, and of all that which passes under the notion of the most abstracted and sublime learning, in all which one shall scarce find any question handled in such a manner as does not suppose their existence in the mind, and that it is well acquainted with them.

7. It is agreed on all hands that the qualities or modes of things do never really exist each of them apart by itself, and separated from all others, but are mixed, as it were, and blended together, several in the same object. But, we are told, the mind being able to consider each quality singly, or abstracted from those other qualities with which it is united, does by that means frame to itself abstract ideas. For example, there is perceived by sight an object extended, coloured, and moved: this mixed or compound idea the mind resolving into its simple, constituent parts, and viewing each by itself, exclusive of the rest, does frame the abstract ideas of extension, colour, and motion. Not that it is possible for colour or motion to exist without extension; but only that the mind can frame to itself by *abstraction* the idea of colour exclusive of extension, and of motion exclusive of both colour and extension.

8. Again, the mind having observed that in the particular extensions perceived by sense there is something common and alike in all, and some other things peculiar, as this or that figure or magnitude, which

distinguish them one from another; it considers apart or singles out by itself that which is common, making thereof a most abstract idea of extension, which is neither line, surface, nor solid, nor has any figure or magnitude, but is an idea entirely prescinded from all these. So likewise the mind, by leaving out of the particular colours perceived by sense that which distinguishes them one from another, and retaining that only which is common to all, makes an idea of colour in abstract which is neither red, nor blue, nor white, nor any other determinate colour. And, in like manner, by considering motion abstractedly not only from the body moved, but likewise from the figure it describes, and all particular directions and velocities, the abstract idea of motion is framed; which equally corresponds to all particular motions whatsoever that may be perceived by sense.

9. And as the mind frames to itself abstract ideas of qualities or modes, so does it, by the same precision or mental separation, attain abstract ideas of the more compounded beings which include several coexistent qualities. For example, the mind having observed that Peter, James, and John resemble each other in certain common agreements of shape and other qualities, leaves out of the complex or compounded idea it has of Peter, James, and any other particular man, that which is peculiar to each, retaining only what is common to all, and so makes an abstract idea wherein all the particulars equally partake—abstracting entirely from and cutting off all those circumstances and differences which might determine it to any particular existence. And after this manner it is said we come by the abstract idea of man, or, if you please, humanity, or human nature; wherein it is true there is in-

cluded colour, because there is no man but has some
colour, but then it can be neither white, nor black, nor
any particular colour, because there is no one particular
colour wherein all men partake. So likewise there is included stature, but then it is neither tall stature, nor
low stature, nor yet middle stature, but something
abstracted from all these. And so of the rest. Moreover, their being a great variety of other creatures
that partake in some parts, but not all, of the complex
idea of man, the mind, leaving out those parts which
are peculiar to men, and retaining those only which
are common to all the living creatures, frames the
idea of *animal*, which abstracts not only from all particular men, but also all birds, beasts, fishes, and in-
sects. The constituent parts of the abstract idea of
animal are body, life, sense, and spontaneous motion.
By *body* is meant body without any particular shape
or figure, there being no one shape or figure common
to all animals, without covering, either of hair, or
feathers, or scales, &c., nor yet naked: hair, feathers,
scales, and nakedness being the distinguishing properties of particular animals, and for that reason left
out of the *abstract idea.* Upon the same account the
spontaneous motion must be neither walking, nor fly-
ing, nor creeping; it is nevertheless a motion, but
what that motion is it is not easy to conceive.

10.   Whether others have this wonderful faculty
of abstracting their ideas, they best can tell: for myself [I dare be confident I have it not],* I find indeed
I have a faculty of imagining, or representing to myself, the ideas of those particular things I have per-

----

*The bracketed words were omitted in the second edition
(1734).

ceived, and of variously compounding and dividing them. I can imagine a man with two heads, or the upper parts of a man joined to the body of a horse. I can consider the hand, the eye, the nose, each by itself abstracted or separated from the rest of the body. But then whatever hand or eye I imagine, it must have some particular shape and colour. Likewise the idea of man that I frame to myself must be either of a white, or a black, or a tawny, a straight, or a crooked, a tall, or a low, or a middle-sized man. I cannot by any effort of thought conceive the abstract idea above described. And it is equally impossible for me to form the abstract idea of motion distinct from the body moving, and which is neither swift nor slow, curvilinear nor rectilinear; and the like may be said of all other abstract general ideas whatsoever. To be plain, I own myself able to abstract in one sense, as when I consider some particular parts or qualities separated from others, with which, though they are united in some object, yet it is possible they may really exist without them. But I deny that I can abstract from one another, or conceive separately, those qualities which it is impossible should exist so separated; or that I can frame a general notion, by abstracting from particulars in the manner aforesaid—which last are the two proper acceptations of *abstraction*. And there are grounds to think most men will acknowledge themselves to be in my case. The generality of men which are simple and illiterate never pretend to *abstract notions*. It is said they are difficult and not to be attained without pains and study; we may therefore reasonably conclude that, if such there be, they are confined only to the learned.

11. I proceed to examine what can be alleged in

defence of the doctrine of abstraction, and try if I can discover what it is that inclines the men of speculation to embrace an opinion so remote from common sense as that seems to be. There has been a late deservedly esteemed philosopher who, no doubt, has given it very much countenance, by seeming to think the having abstract general ideas is what puts the widest difference in point of understanding betwixt man and beast. "The having of general ideas," saith he, "is that which puts a perfect distinction betwixt man and brutes, and is an excellency which the faculties of brutes do by no means attain unto. For, it is evident we observe no foot-steps in them of making use of general signs for universal ideas; from which we have reason to imagine that they have not the faculty of abstracting, or making general ideas, since they have no use of words or any other general signs." And a little after: "Therefore, I think, we may suppose that it is in this that the species of brutes are discriminated from men, and it is that proper difference wherein they are wholly separated, and which at last widens to so wide a distance. For, if they have any ideas at all, and are not bare machines (as some would have them), we cannot deny them to have some reason. It seems as evident to me that they do, some of them, in certain instances reason as that they have sense; but it is only in particular ideas, just as they receive them from their senses. They are the best of them tied up within those narrow bounds, and have not (as I think) the faculty to enlarge them by any kind of abstraction."—"Essay on Human Understanding," B. ii. ch. 11. s.10 and 11. I readily agree with this learned author, that the faculties of brutes can by no means attain to abstraction. But then if this be made the distinguishing property of that sort of animals, I fear a great many of those that pass for men must be reckoned into their number. The reason that is here assigned why we have no grounds to think brutes have abstract general ideas is, that we observe in them no use of words or any other general signs; which is built on this supposition—that the making use of words implies the having general ideas. From which it follows that men who use language are able to abstract or generalize their ideas. That this is the sense and arguing of the author will further appear by his answering the question he in another place puts: "Since all things that exist are only particulars, how come we by general terms?" His answer is: "Words become general by being made the signs of general ideas."— "Essay on Human Understanding," B. iii. ch. 3 s. 6. But* it seems that a word becomes general by being made the sign, not of an abstract general idea, but of several particular ideas, any one of which it indifferently suggests to the mind. For example, when it is said "the change of motion is proportional to the impressed force," or that "whatever has extension is divisible," these propositions are to be understood of motion and extension in general; and nevertheless it will not follow that they suggest to my thoughts an idea of motion without a body moved, or any determinate direction and velocity, or that I must conceive an abstract general idea of extension, which is neither line, surface, nor solid, neither great nor small, black, white, nor red, nor of any other determinate colour.

---

*In the first edition (1710) this sentence began as follows: "To this I cannot assent being of opinion that a word becomes general," &c.

It is only implied that whatever particular motion I consider, whether it be swift or slow, perpendicular, horizontal, or oblique, or in whatever object, the axiom concerning it holds equally true. As does the other of every particular extension, it matters not whether line, surface, or solid, whether of this or that magnitude or figure.

12. By observing how ideas become general we may the better judge how words are made so. And here it is to be noted that I do not deny absolutely there are general ideas, but only that there are any *abstract* general ideas; for, in the passages we have quoted wherein there is mention of general ideas, it is always supposed that they are formed by abstraction, after the manner set forth in sections 8 and 9. Now, if we will annex a meaning to our words, and speak only of what we can conceive, I believe we shall acknowledge that an idea which, considered in itself, is particular, becomes general by being made to represent or stand for all other particular ideas of the same sort. To make this plain by an example, suppose a geometrician is demonstrating the method of cutting a line in two equal parts. He draws, for instance, a black line of an inch in length: this, which in itself is a particular line, is nevertheless with regard to its signification general, since, as it is there used, it represents all particular lines whatsoever; so that what is demonstrated of it is demonstrated of all lines, or, in other words, of a line in general. And, as that *particular* line becomes general by being made a sign, so the *name* "line," which taken absolutely is particular, by being a sign is made general. And as the former owes its generality not to its being the sign of an abstract or general line, but of all particular right lines that may pos-

sibly exist, so the latter must be thought to derive its generality from the same cause, namely, the various particular lines which it indifferently denotes.

13. To give the reader a yet clearer view of the nature of abstract ideas, and the uses they are thought necessary to, I shall add one more passage out of the "Essay on Human Understanding," which is as follows: "*Abstract ideas* are not so obvious or easy to children or the yet unexercised mind as particular ones. If they seem so to grown men it is only because by constant and familiar use they are made so. For, when we nicely reflect upon them, we shall find that general ideas are fictions and contrivances of the mind, that carry difficulty with them, and do not so easily offer themselves as we are apt to imagine. For example, does it not require some pains and skill to form the general idea of a triangle (which is yet none of the most abstract, comprehensive, and difficult); for it must be neither oblique nor rectangle, neither equilateral, equicrural, nor scalenon, but *all and none* of these at once? In effect, it is something imperfect that cannot exist, an idea wherein some parts of several different and *inconsistent* ideas are put together. It is true the mind in this imperfect state has need of such ideas, and makes all the haste to them it can, for the conveniency of communication and enlargement of knowledge, to both which it is naturally very much inclined. But yet one has reason to suspect such ideas are marks of our imperfection. At least this is enough to show that the most abstract and general ideas are not those that the mind is first and most easily acquainted with, nor such as its earliest knowledge is conversant about."—B. iv. ch. 7. s. 9. If any man has the faculty of framing in his mind such an idea of a

triangle as is here described, it is in vain to pretend
to dispute him out of it, nor would I go about it. All
I desire is that the reader would fully and certainly
inform himself whether he has such an idea or no.
And this, methinks, can be no hard task for anyone to
perform. What more easy than for anyone to look a
little into his own thoughts, and there try whether he
has, or can attain to have, an idea that shall correspond
with the description that is here given of the general
idea of a triangle, which is "neither oblique nor rectangle, equilateral, equicrural nor scalenon, but all and
none of these at once?"

14. Much is here said of the difficulty that abstract
ideas carry with them, and the pains and skill requisite
to the forming them. And it is on all hands agreed
that there is need of great toil and labour of the mind,
to emancipate our thoughts from particular objects,
and raise them to those sublime speculations that are
conversant about abstract ideas. From all which the
natural consequence should seem to be, that so difficult
a thing as the forming abstract ideas was not necessary for *communication,* which is so easy and familiar
to all sorts of men. But, we are told, if they seem
obvious and easy to grown men, it is only because by
constant and familiar use they are made so. Now, I
would fain know at what time it is men are employed
in surmounting that difficulty, and furnishing themselves with those necessary helps for discourse. It
cannot be when they are grown up, for then it seems
they are not conscious of any such painstaking; it
remains therefore to be the business of their childhood.
And surely the great and multiplied labour of framing abstract notions will be found a hard task for that
tender age. Is it not a hard thing to imagine that a

couple of children cannot prate together of their sugar-plums and rattles and the rest of their little trinkets, till they have first tacked together numberless inconsistencies, and so framed in their minds abstract general ideas, and annexed them to every common name they make use of?

15. Nor do I think them a whit more needful for the *enlargement of knowledge* than for *communication*. It is, I know, a point much insisted on, that all knowledge and demonstration are about universal notions, to which I fully agree: but then it doth not appear to me that those notions are formed by abstraction in the manner premised—*universality*, so far as I can comprehend, not consisting in the absolute, positive nature or conception of anything, but in the relation it bears to the particulars signified or represented by it; by virtue whereof it is that things, names, or notions, being in their own nature *particular*, are rendered *universal*. Thus, when I demonstrate any proposition concerning triangles, it is to be supposed that I have in view the universal idea of a triangle; which ought not to be understood as if I could frame an idea of a triangle which was neither equilateral, nor scalenon, nor equicrural; but only that the particular triangle I consider, whether of this or that sort it matters not, doth equally stand for and represent all rectilinear triangles whatsoever, and is in that sense *universal*. All which seems very plain and not to include any difficulty in it.

16. But here it will be demanded, how we can know any proposition to be true of all particular triangles, except we have first seen it demonstrated of the abstract idea of a triangle which equally agrees to all? For, because a property may be demonstrated to agree

to some one particular triangle, it will not thence follow that it equally belongs to any other triangle, which in all respects is not the same with it. For example, having demonstrated that the three angles of an isoceles rectangular triangle are equal to two right ones, I cannot therefore conclude this affection agrees to all other triangles which have neither a right angle nor two equal sides. It seems therefore that, to be certain this proposition is universally true, we must either make a particular demonstration for every particular triangle, which is impossible, or once for all demonstrate it of the abstract idea of a triangle, in which all the particulars do indifferently partake and by which they are all equally represented. To which I answer, that, though the idea I have in view whilst I make the demonstration be, for instance, that of an isosceles rectangular triangle whose sides are of a determinate length, I may nevertheless be certain it extends to all other rectilinear triangles, of what sort or bigness soever. And that because neither the right angle, nor the equality, nor determinate length of the sides are at all concerned in the demonstration. It is true the diagram I have in view includes all these particulars, but then there is not the least mention made of them in the proof of the proposition. It is not said the three angles are equal to two right ones, because one of them is a right angle, or because the sides comprehending it are of the same length. Which sufficiently shows that the right angle might have been oblique, and the sides unequal, and for all that the demonstration have held good. And for this reason it is that I conclude that to be true of any obliquangular or scalenon which I had demonstrated of a particular right-angled equicrural triangle, and not because I demonstrated the proposition of the abstract idea of a triangle.   [And here it must be acknowledged that a man may consider a figure merely as triangular, without attending to the particular qualities of the angles, or relations of the sides.   So far he may abstract; but this will never prove that he can frame an abstract, general, inconsistent idea of a triangle.   In like manner we may consider Peter so far forth as man, or so far forth as animal, without framing the forementioned abstract idea, either of man or of animal, inasmuch as all that is perceived is not considered.*]

17. It were an endless as well as an useless thing to trace the Schoolmen, those great masters of abstraction, through all the manifold inextricable labyrinths of error and dispute which their doctrine of abstract natures and notions seems to have led them into.   What bickerings and controversies, and what a learned dust have been raised about those matters, and what mighty advantage has been from thence derived to mankind, are things at this day too clearly known to need being insisted on.   And it had been well if the ill effects of that doctrine were confined to those only who make the most avowed profession of it.   When men consider the great pains, industry, and parts that have for so many ages been laid out on the cultivation and advancement of the sciences, and that notwithstanding all this the far greater part of them remains full of darkness and uncertainty, and disputes that are like never to have an end, and even those that are thought to be supported by the most clear and cogent demonstrations contain in them paradoxes which are perfectly irreconcilable

---

*The bracketed sentences were inserted in the last or 1734 edition.

to the understandings of men, and that, taking all together, a very small portion of them does supply any
real benefit to mankind, otherwise than by being an
innocent diversion and amusement—I say the consideration of all this is apt to throw them into a despondency
and perfect contempt of all study. But this may perhaps cease upon a view of the false principles that have
obtained in the world, amongst all which there is none,
methinks, hath a more wide and extended sway over
the thoughts of speculative men than this of *abstract*
general ideas.

18. I come now to consider the *source* of this prevailing notion, and that seems to me to be language.
And surely nothing of less extent than reason itself
could have been the source of an opinion so universally
received. The truth of this appears as from other
reasons so also from the plain confession of the ablest
patrons of abstract ideas, who acknowledge that they
are made in order to naming; from which it is a clear
consequence that if there had been no such thing as
speech or universal signs there never had been any
thought of abstraction. See B. iii, ch. 6, s. 39, and
elsewhere of the "Essay on Human Understanding."
Let us examine the manner wherein words have contributed to the origin of that mistake.—First then, it
is thought that every name has, or ought to have, one
only precise and settled signification, which inclines
men to think there are certain abstract, determinate ideas
that constitute the true and only immediate signification
of each general name; and that it is by the mediation
of these abstract ideas that a general name comes to
signify any particular thing. Whereas, in truth, there
is no such thing as one precise and definite signification annexed to any general name, they all signifying

indifferently a great number of particular ideas. All which doth evidently follow from what has been already said, and will clearly appear to anyone by a little reflexion. To this it will be objected that every name that has a definition is thereby restrained to one certain signification. For example, a triangle is defined to be "a plain surface comprehended by three right lines," by which that name is limited to denote one certain idea and no other. To which I answer, that in the definition it is not said whether the surface be great or small, black or white, nor whether the sides are long or short, equal or unequal, nor with what angles they are inclined to each other; in all which there may be great variety, and consequently there is no one settled idea which limits the signification of the word triangle. It is one thing for to keep a name constantly to the same definition, and another to make it stand everywhere for the same idea; the one is necessary, the other useless and impracticable.

19. But, to give a farther account how words came to produce the doctrine of abstract ideas, it must be observed that it is a received opinion that language has no other end but the communicating our ideas, and that every significant name stands for an idea. This being so, and it being withal certain that names which yet are not thought altogether insignificant do not always mark out particular conceivable ideas, it is straightway concluded that they stand for abstract notions. That there are many names in use amongst speculative men which do not always suggest to others determinate, particular ideas, or in truth anything at all, is what nobody will deny. And a little attention will discover that it is not necessary (even in the strictest reasonings) significant names which stand for ideas should, every time they are

used, excite in the understanding the ideas they are
made to stand for—in reading and discoursing, names
being for the most part used as letters are in Algebra,
in which, though a particular quantity b‿ marked by
each letter, yet to proceed right it is not requisite that
in every step each letter suggest to your thoughts that
particular quantity it was appointed to stand for.

20. Besides, the communicating of ideas marked by
words is not the chief and only end of language, as is
commonly supposed. There are other ends, as the rais-
ing of some passion, the exciting to or deterring from
an action, the putting the mind in some particular disposition—to which the former is in many cases barely
subservient, and sometimes entirely omitted, when these
can be obtained without it, as I think does not unfre-
quently happen in the familiar use of language. I
entreat the reader to reflect with himself, and see if it
doth not often happen, either in hearing or reading a
discourse, that the passions of fear, love, hatred, ad-
miration, disdain, and the like, arise immediately in his
mind upon the perception of certain words, without any
ideas coming between. At first, indeed, the words
might have occasioned ideas that were fitting to produce
those emotions; but, if I mistake not, it will be found
that, when language is once grown familiar, the hearing
of the sounds or sight of the characters is oft immediately attended with those passions which at first were
wont to be produced by the intervention of ideas that
are now quite omitted. May we not, for example, be
affected with the promise of a *good thing,* though we
have not an idea of what it is? Or is not the being
threatened with danger sufficient to excite a dread,
though we think not of any particular evil likely to befal
us, nor yet frame to ourselves an idea of danger in ab-

stract? If any one shall join ever so little reflexion of
his own to what has been said, I believe that it will
evidently appear to him that general names are often
used in the propriety of language without the speaker's
designing them for marks of ideas in his own, which
he would have them raise in the mind of the hearer.
Even proper names themselves do not seem always
spoken with a design to bring into our view the ideas
of those individuals that are supposed to be marked by
them. For example, when a schoolman tells me
"Aristotle hath said it," all I conceive he means by it
is to dispose me to embrace his opinion with the defer-
ence and submission which custom has annexed to that
name. And this effect is often so instantly produced
in the minds of those who are accustomed to resign
their judgment to authority of that philosopher, as it
is impossible any idea either of his person, writings, or
reputation should go before. [So close and immediate a
connexion may custom establish betwixt the very word
Aristotle and the motions of assent and reverence in the
minds of some men.]* Innumerable examples of this
kind may be given, but why should I insist on those
things which every one's experience will, I doubt not,
plentifully suggest unto him?

21. We have, I think, shewn the impossibility of
Abstract Ideas. We have considered what has been
said for them by their ablest patrons; and endeavored
to show they are of no use for those ends to which they
are thought necessary. And lastly, we have traced
them to the source from whence they flow, which appears evidently to be language.—It cannot be denied

---

*The bracketed words were omitted in the second edition
(1734).

that words are of excellent use, in that by their means
all that stock of knowledge which has been purchased
by the joint labours of inquisitive men in all ages and
nations may be drawn into the view and made the pos-
session of one single person.   [But at the same time it
must be owned that most parts of knowledge have been
strangely perplexed and darkened by the abuse of
words, and general ways of speech wherein they are
delivered. Since therefore words are so apt to impose on
the understanding,]* whatever ideas I consider, I shall
endeavour to take them bare and naked into my view,
keeping out of my thoughts so far as I am able, those
names which long and constant use hath so strictly
united with them; from which I may expect to derive
the following advantages :—

22. *First,* I shall be sure to get clear of all controversies purely verbal—the springing up of which weeds
in almost all the sciences has been a main hindrance to
the growth of true and sound knowledge. *Secondly,*
this seems to be a sure way to extricate myself out of
that fine and subtle net of *abstract ideas* which has so
miserably perplexed and entangled the minds of men;
and that with this peculiar circumstance, that by how
much the finer and more curious was the wit of any
man, by so much the deeper was he likely to be ensnared
and faster held therein. *Thirdly,* so long as I confine

---

*In the first edition (1710) the bracketed passage read as
follows: "But most parts of knowledge have been so strangely
perplexed and darkened by the abuse of words, and general
ways of speech wherein they are delivered, that it may almost
be made a question whether language has contributed more to
hindrance or advancement of the sciences. Since therefore
words are so apt to impose on the understanding, I am resolved in my inquiries to make as little use of them as possibly I can : whatever ideas I consider," &c.

my thoughts to my own ideas divested of words, I do not see how I can easily be mistaken. The objects I consider, I clearly and adequately know. I cannot be deceived in thinking I have an idea which I have not. It is not possible for me to imagine that any of my own ideas are alike or unlike that are not truly so. To discern the agreements or disagreements there are between my ideas, to see what ideas are included in any compound idea and what not, there is nothing more requisite than an attentive preception of what passes in my own understanding.

23. But the attainment of all these advantages doth presuppose an entire deliverance from the deception of words, which I dare hardly promise myself; so difficult a thing it is to dissolve an union so early begun, and confirmed by so long a habit as that betwixt words and ideas. Which difficulty seems to have been very much increased by the doctrine of *abstraction.* For, so long as men thought abstract ideas were annexed to their words, it doth not seem strange that they should use words for ideas—it being found an impracticable thing to lay aside the word, and retain the *abstract* idea in the mind, which in itself was perfectly inconceivable. This seems to me the principal cause why those men who have so emphatically recommended to others the laying aside all use of words in their meditations, and contemplating their bare ideas, have yet failed to perform it themselves. Of late many have been very sensible of the absurd opinons and insignificant disputes which grow out of the abuse of words. And, in order to remedy these evils, they advise well, that we attend to the ideas signified, and draw off our attention from the words which signify them. But, how good soever this advice may be they have given others, it is plain they

could not have a due regard to it themselves, so long as they thought the only immediate use of words was to signify ideas, and that the immediate signification of every general name was a determinate abstract idea.

24. But, these being known to be mistakes, a man may with greater ease prevent his being imposed on by words. He that knows he has no other than *particular* ideas, will not puzzle himself in vain to find out and conceive the *abstract* idea annexed to any name. And he that knows names do not always stand for ideas will spare himself the labour of looking for ideas where there are none to be had. It were, therefore, to be wished that everyone would use his utmost endeavours to obtain a clear view of the ideas he would consider, separating from them all that dress and incumbrance of words which so much contribute to blind the judgment and divide the attention. In vain do we extend our view into the heavens and pry into the entrails of the earth, in vain do we consult the writings of learned men and trace the dark footsteps of antiquity—we need only draw the curtain of words, to hold the fairest tree of knowledge, whose fruit is excellent, and within the reach of our hand.

25. Unless we take care to clear the First Principles of Knowledge from the embarras and delusion of words, we may make infinite reasonings upon them to no purpose; we may draw consequences from consequences, and be never the wiser. The farther we go, we shall only lose ourselves the more irrecoverably, and be the deeper entangled in difficulties and mistakes. Whoever therefore designs to read the following sheets, I entreat him to make my words the occasion of his own thinking, and endeavour to attain the same train of thoughts in reading that I had in writing them. By this

means it will be easy for him to discover the truth or falsity of what I say. He will be out of all danger of being deceived by my words, and I do not see how he can be led into an error by considering his own naked, undisguised ideas.

Of the Principles of Human Knowledge

[PART I.*]

It is evident to any one who takes a survey of the *objects* of human knowledge, that they are either ideas actually imprinted on the senses; or else such as are perceived by attending to the passions and operations of the mind; or lastly, ideas formed by help of memory and imagination—either compounding, dividing, or barely representing those originally perceived in the aforesaid ways. By sight I have the ideas of light and colours, with their several degrees and variations. By touch I perceive hard and soft, heat and cold, motion and resistance, and of all these more and less either as to quantity or degree. Smelling furnishes me with odours; the palate with tastes; and hearing conveys sounds to the mind in all their variety of tone and composition. And as several of these are observed to accompany each other, they come to be marked by one name, and so to be reputed as one thing. Thus, for example, a certain colour, taste, smell, figure and con-

*Omitted from the title-page of the second edition (1734), but retained at this place. The promised Second Part never appeared.

sistence having been observed to go together, are accounted one distinct thing, signified by the name *apple;* other collections of ideas constitute a stone, a tree, a book, and the like sensible things—which as they are pleasing or disagreeable excite the passions of love, hatred, joy, grief, and so forth.

2. But, besides all that endless variety of ideas or objects of knowledge, there is likewise something which knows or perceives them, and exercises divers operations, as willing, imagining, remembering, about them. This perceiving, active being is what I call *mind, spirit, soul,* or *myself.* By which words I do not denote any one of my ideas, but a thing entirely distinct from them, wherein, they exist, or, which is the same thing, whereby they are perceived—for the existence of an idea consists in being perceived.

3. That neither our thoughts, nor passions, nor ideas formed by the imagination, exist without the mind, is what everybody will allow. And it seems no less evident that the various sensations or ideas imprinted on the sense, however blended or combined together (that is, whatever objects they compose), cannot exist otherwise than in a mind perceiving them.—I think an intuitive knowledge may be obtained of this by any one that shall attend to what is meant by the term *exists,* when applied to sensible things. The table I write on I say exists, that is, I see and feel it; and if I were out of my study I should say it existed—meaning thereby that if I was in my study I might perceive it, or that some other spirit actually does perceive it. There was an odour, that is, it was smelt; there was a sound, that is, it was heard; a colour or figure, and it was perceived

by sight or touch. This is all that I can understand by these and the like expressions. For as to what is said of the absolute existence of unthinking things without any relation to their being perceived, that seems perfectly unintelligible. Their *esse* is *percipi*, nor is it possible they should have any existence out of the minds or thinking things which perceive them.

4. It is indeed an opinion strangely prevailing amongst men, that houses, mountains, rivers, and in a word all sensible objects, have an existence, natural or real, distinct from their being perceived by the understanding. But, with how great an assurance and acquiescence soever this principle may be entertained in the world, yet whoever shall find in his heart to call it in question may, if I mistake not, perceive it to involve a manifest contradiction. For, what are the fore-mentioned objects but the things we perceive by sense? and what do we perceive besides our own ideas or sensations? and is it not plainly repugnant that any one of these, or any combination of them, should exist unperceived?

5. If we thoroughly examine this tenet it will, perhaps, be found at bottom to depend on the doctrine of *abstract ideas*. For can there be a nicer strain of abstraction than to distinguish the existence of sensible objects from their being perceived, so as to conceive them existing unperceived? Light and colours, heat and cold, extension and figures—in a word the things we see and feel—what are they but so many sensations, notions, ideas, or impressions on the sense? and is it possible to separate, even in thought, any of these from perception? For my part, I might as easily divide a thing from itself. I may, indeed, divide in my thoughts,

or conceive apart from each other, those things which, perhaps I never perceived by sense so divided. Thus, I imagine the trunk of a human body without the limbs, or conceive the smell of a rose without thinking on the rose itself. So far, I will not deny, I can abstract—if that may properly be called *abstraction* which extends only to the conceiving separately such objects as it is possible may really exist or be actually perceived asunder. But my conceiving or imagining power does not extend beyond the possibility of real existence or perception. Hence, as it is impossible for me to see or feel anything without an actual sensation of that thing, so is it impossible for me to conceive in my thoughts any sensible thing or object distinct from the sensation or perception of it. [In truth, the object and the sensation are the same thing, and cannot therefore be abstracted from each other.]*

6. Some truths there are so near and obvious to the mind that a man need only open his eyes to see them. Such I take this important one to be, viz., that all the choir of heaven and furniture of the earth, in a word all those bodies which compose the mighty frame of the world, have not any subsistence without a mind, that their *being* is to be perceived or known ; that consequently so long as they are not actually perceived by me, or do not exist in my mind or that of any other created spirit, they must either have no existence at all, or else subsist in the mind of some Eternal Spirit—it being perfectly unintelligible, and involving all the absurdity of abstraction, to attribute to any single part of them an existence independent of a spirit. [To be convinced of which, the reader need only reflect, and try to sepa-

---

*Omitted from the second edition.

rate in his own thoughts the *being* of a sensible thing from its *being perceived.*]*

7. From what has been said it follows there is not any other Substance than *Spirit,* or that which perceives. But, for the fuller proof of this point, let it be considered the sensible qualities are colour, figure, motion, smell, taste, etc., *i. e.* the ideas perceived by sense. Now, for an idea to exist in an unperceiving thing is a manifest contradiction, for to have an idea is all one as to perceive; that therefore wherein colour, figure, and the like qualities exist must perceive them; hence it is clear there can be no unthinking substance or *substratum* of those ideas.

8. But, say you, though the ideas themselves do not exist without the mind, yet there may be things like them, whereof they are copies or resemblances, which things exist without the mind in an unthinking substance. I answer, an idea can be like nothing but an idea; a colour or figure can be like nothing but another colour or figure. If we look but never so little into our thoughts, we shall find it impossible for us to conceive a likeness except only between our ideas. Again, I ask whether those supposed originals or external things, of which our ideas are the pictures or representations, be themselves perceivable or no? If they are, then they are ideas and we have gained our point; but if you say they are not, I appeal to any one whether it be sense to as-

*In the first edition the bracketed sentence is not found, but in its place we have the following: "To make this appear with all the light and evidence of an Axiom, it seems sufficient if I can but awaken the reflexion of the reader, that he may take an impartial view of his own meaning, and turn his thoughts upon the subject itself, free and disengaged from all embarras of words and prepossession in favour of received mistakes."

sert a colour is like something which is invisible; hard
or soft, like something which is intangible; and so of
the rest.

9. Some there are who make a distinction betwixt
primary and *secondary* qualities. By the former they
mean extension, figure, motion, rest, solidity or impene-
trability, and number; by the latter they denote all other
sensible qualities, as colours, sounds, tastes, and so
forth. The ideas we have of these they acknowledge not
to be the resemblances of anything existing without the
mind, or unperceived, but they will have our ideas of
the primary qualities to be patterns or images of things
which exist without the mind, in an unthinking substance which they call Matter. By Matter, therefore,
we are to understand an inert, senseless substance, in
which extension, figure, and motion do actually subsist.
But it is evident from what we have already shown,
that extension, figure, and motion are only ideas existing in the mind, and that an idea can be like nothing
but another idea, and that consequently neither they nor
their archetypes can exist in an unperceiving substance.
Hence, it is plain that the very notion of what is called
Matter or *corporeal substance,* involves a contradiction
in it.*

10. They who assert that figure, motion, and the
rest of the primary or original qualities do exist without
the mind in unthinking substances, do at the same time

*In the first edition the following passage ended this sec-
tion: "Insomuch that I should not think it necessary to spend
more time in exposing its absurdity. But, because the tenet
of the existence of Matter seems to have taken so deep a root
in the minds of philosophers, and draws after it so many ill
consequences, I choose rather to be thought prolix and tedious
than omit anything that might conduce to the full discovery
and extirpation of that prejudice."

acknowledge that colours, sounds, heat, cold, and such-like secondary qualities, do not—which they tell us are sensations existing in the mind alone, that depend on and are occasioned by the different size, texture, and motion of the minute particles of matter. This they take for an undoubted truth, which they can demonstrate beyond all exception. Now, if it be certain that those original qualities are inseparably united with the other sensible qualities, and not, even in thought, capable of being abstracted from them, it plainly follows that they exist only in the mind. But I desire any one to reflect and try whether he can, by any abstraction of thought, conceive the extension and motion of a body without all other sensible qualities. For my own part, I see evidently that it is not in my power to frame an idea of a body extended and moving, but I must withal give it some colour or other sensible quality which is acknowledged to exist only in the mind. In short, extension, figure, and motion, abstracted from all other qualities, are inconceivable. Where therefore the other sensible qualities are, there must these be also, to wit, in the mind and nowhere else.

11. Again, *great* and *small, swift* and *slow,* are allowed to exist nowhere without the mind, being entirely relative, and changing as the frame or position of the organs of sense varies. The extension therefore which exists without the mind is neither great nor small, the motion neither swift nor slow, that is, they are nothing at all. But, say you, they are extension in general, and motion in general: thus we see how much the tenet of extended movable substances existing without the mind depends on the strange doctrine of *abstract ideas.* And here I cannot but remark how nearly the vague and indeterminate description of Matter or

corporeal substance, which the modern philosophers are run into by their own principles, resembles that antiquated and so much ridiculed notion of *materia prima*, to be met with in Aristotle and his followers. Without extension solidity cannot be conceived; since therefore it has been shewn that extension exists not in an unthinking substance, the same must also be true of solidity.

12. That number is entirely the creature of the mind, even though the other qualities be allowed to exist without, will be evident to whoever considers that the same thing bears a different denomination of number as the mind views it with different respects. Thus, the same extension is one, or three, or thirty-six, according as the mind considers it with reference to a yard, a foot, or an inch. Number is so visibly relative, and dependent on men's understanding, that it is strange to think how any one should give it an absolute existence without the mind. We say one book, one page, one line, etc.; all these are equally units, though some contain several of the others. And in each instance, it is plain, the unit relates to some particular combination of ideas arbitrarily put together by the mind.

13. Unity I know some will have to be a simple or uncompounded idea, accompanying all other ideas into the mind. That I have any such idea answering the word *unity* I do not find; and if I had, methinks I could not miss finding it: on the contrary, it should be the most familiar to my understanding, since it is said to accompany all other ideas, and to be perceived by all the ways of sensation and reflexion. To say no more, it is an *abstract idea*.

14. I shall farther add, that, after the same manner as modern philosophers prove certain sensible qualities

to have no existence in Matter, or without the mind, the same thing may be likewise proved of all other sensible qualities whatsoever. Thus, for instance, it is said that heat and cold are affections only of the mind, and not at all patterns of real beings, existing in the corporeal substances which excite them, for that the same body which appears cold to one hand seems warm to another. Now, why may we not as well argue that figure and extension are not patterns or resemblances of qualities existing in Matter, because to the same eye at different stations, or eyes of a different texture at the same station, they appear various, and cannot therefore be the images of anything settled and determinate without the mind? Again, it is proved that sweetness is not really in the sapid thing, because the thing remaining unaltered the sweetness is changed into bitter, as in case of a fever or otherwise vitiated palate. Is it not as reasonable to say that motion is not without the mind, since if the succession of ideas in the mind become swifter, the motion, it is acknowledged, shall appear slower without any alteration in any external object?*

15. In short, let any one consider those arguments which are thought manifestly to prove that colours and taste exist only in the mind, and he shall find they may with equal force be brought to prove the same thing of extension, figure, and motion. Though it must be confessed this method of arguing does not so much prove that there is no extension or colour in an outward object, as that we do not know by sense which is the true extension or colour of the object. But the arguments foregoing plainly show it to be impossible that any colour or extension at all, or other sensible quality

---

*In the first edition the last seven words read: "without **any** external alteration."

whatsoever, should exist in an unthinking subject without the mind, or in truth, that there should be any such thing as an outward object.

16.   But let us examine a little the received opinon. —It is said extension is a mode or accident of Matter, and that Matter is the *substratum* that supports it. Now I desire that you would explain to me what is meant by Matter's *supporting* extension.   Say you, I have no idea of Matter and therefore cannot explain it. I answer, though you have no positive, yet, if you have any meaning at all, you must at least have a relative idea of Matter; though you know not what it is, yet you must be supposed to know what relation it bears to accidents, and what is meant by its supporting them. It is evident "support" cannot here be taken in its usual or literal sense—as when we say that pillars support a building; in what sense therefore must it be taken?*

17.   If we inquire into what the most accurate philosophers declare themselves to mean by *material substance,* we shall find them acknowledge they have no other meaning annexed to those sounds but the idea of Being in general, together with the relative notion of its supporting accidents.   The general idea of Being appeareth to me the most abstract and incomprehensible of all other; and as for its supporting accidents, this, as we have just now observed, cannot be understood in the common sense of those words; it must therefore be taken in some other sense, but what that is they do not explain.   So that when I consider the two parts or branches which make the signification of the words *material substance,* I am convinced there is no distinct

---

*In the first edition the following sentence occurred here: "For my part, I am not able to discover any sense at all that can be aplicable to it."

meaning annexed to them. But why should we trouble ourselves any farther, in discussing this material *substratum* or support of figure and motion, and other sensible qualities? Does it not suppose they have an existence without the mind? And is not this a direct repugnancy, and altogether inconceivable?

18. But, though it were possible that solid, figured, movable substances may exist without the mind, corresponding to the ideas we have of bodies, yet how is it possible for us to know this? Either we must know it by sense or by reason. As for our senses, by them we have the knowledge only of our sensations, ideas, or those things that are immediately perceived by sense, call them what you will: but they do not inform us that things exist without the mind, or unperceived, like to those which are perceived. This the materialists themselves acknowledge. It remains therefore that if we have any knowledge at all of external things, it must be by reason, inferring their existence from what is immediately perceived by sense. But what reason can induce us to believe the existence of bodies without the mind, from what we perceive, since the very patrons of Matter themselves do not pretend there is any necessary connexion betwixt them and our ideas? I say it is granted on all hands (and what happens in dreams, phrensies, and the like, puts it beyond dispute) that it is possible we might be affected with all the ideas we have now, though there were no bodies existing without resembling them. Hence, it is evident the supposition of external bodies is not necessary for the producing our ideas; since it is granted they are produced sometimes, and might possibly be produced always in the same order, we see them in at present, without their concurrence.

19. But, though we might possibly have all our sensations without them, yet perhaps it may be thought easier to conceive and explain the manner of their production, by supposing external bodies in their likeness rather than otherwise; and so it might be at least probable there are such things as bodies that excite their ideas in our minds. But neither can this be said; for, though we give the materialists their external bodies, they by their own confession are never the nearer knowing how our ideas are produced; since they own themselves unable to comprehend in what manner body can act upon spirit, or how it is possible it should imprint any idea in the mind. Hence it is evident the production of ideas or sensations in our minds can be no reason why we should suppose Matter or corporeal substances, since that is acknowledged to remain equally inexplicable with or without this supposition. If therefore it were possible for bodies to exist without the mind, yet to hold they do so, must needs be a very precarious opinion; since it is to suppose, without any reason at all, that God has created innumerable beings that are entirely useless, and serve to no manner of purpose.

20. In short, if there were external bodies, it is impossible we should ever come to know it; and if there were not, we might have the very same reasons to think there were that we have now. Suppose—what no one can deny possible—an intelligence without the help of external bodies, to be affected with the same train of sensations or ideas that you are, imprinted in the same order and with like vividness in his mind. I ask whether that intelligence hath not all the reason to believe the existence of corporeal substances, represented by his ideas, and exciting them in his mind, that you

can possibly have for believing the same thing? **Of**
this there can be no question—which one consideration
were enough to make any reasonable person suspect
the strength of whatever arguments he may think himself to have, for the existence of bodies without the
mind.

21. Were it necessary to add any farther proof
against the existence of Matter after what has been said,
I could instance several of those errors and difficulties
(not to mention impieties) which have sprung from that
tenet. It has occasioned numberless controversies and
disputes in philosophy, and not a few of far greater
moment in religion. But I shall not enter into the de-
tail of them in this place, as well because I think arguments *a posteriori* are unnecessary for confirming what
has been, if I mistake not, sufficiently demonstrated *a
priori,* as because I shall hereafter find occasion to speak
somewhat of them.

22. I am afraid I have given cause to think I am
needlessly prolix in handling this subject. For, to what
purpose is it to dilate on that which may be demonstrated with the utmost evidence in a line or two, to any
one that is capable of the least reflexion? It is but looking into your own thoughts, and so trying whether you
can conceive it possible for a sound, or figure, or motion, or colour to exist without the mind or unperceived.
This easy trial may perhaps make you see that what
you contend for is a downright contradiction. Insomuch that I am content to put the whole upon this
issue:—If you can but conceive it possible for one extended movable substance, or, in general, for any one
idea, or anything like an idea, to exist otherwise than
in a mind perceiving it, I shall readily give up the cause.

And, as for all that compages of external bodies you contend for, I shall grant you its existence, though you cannot either give me any reason why you believe it exists, or assign any use to it when it is supposed to exist. I say, the bare possibility of your opinions being true shall pass for an argument that it is so.

23. But, say you, surely there is nothing easier than for me to imagine trees, for instance, in a park, or books existing in a closet, and nobody by to perceive them. I answer, you may so, there is no difficulty in it; but what is all this, I beseech you, more than framing in your mind certain ideas which you call books and trees, and the same time omitting to frame the idea of any one that may perceive them? But do not you yourself perceive or think of them all the while? This therefore is nothing to the purpose; it only shews you have the power of imagining or forming ideas in your mind: but it does not shew that you can conceive it possible the objects of your thought may exist without the mind. To make out this, it is necessary that you conceive them existing unconceived or unthought of, which is a manifest repugnancy. When we do our utmost to conceive the existence of external bodies, we are all the while only contemplating our own ideas. But the mind taking no notice of itself, is deluded to think it can and does conceive bodies existing unthought of or without the mind, though at the same time they are apprehended by or exist in itself. A little attention will discover to any one the truth and evidence of what is here said, and make it unnecessary to insist on any other proofs against the existence of *material substance*.

24. [Could men but forbear to amuse themselves with words, we should, I believe, soon come to an

agreement in this point.]* It is very obvious, upon the least inquiry into our thoughts, to know whether it is possible for us to understand what is meant by the *absolute existence of sensible objects in themselves, or without the mind.* To me it is evident those words mark out either a direct contradiction, or else nothing at all. And to convince others of this, I know no readier or fairer way than to entreat they would calmly attend to their own thoughts; and if by this attention the emptiness or repugnancy of those expressions does appear, surely nothing more is requisite for the conviction. It is on this therefore that I insist, to wit, that the absolute existence of unthinking things are words without a meaning, or which include a contradiction. This is what I repeat and inculcate, and earnestly recommend to the attentive thoughts of the reader.

25. All our ideas, sensations, notions, or the things which we perceive, by whatsoever names they may be distinguished, are visibly inactive—there is nothing of power or agency included in them. So that one idea or object of thought cannot produce or make any alteration in another. To be satisfied of the truth of this, there is nothing else requisite but a bare observation of our ideas. For, since they and every part of them exist only in the mind, it follows that there is nothing in them but what is perceived: but whoever shall attend to his ideas, whether of sense or reflexion, will not perceive in them any power or activity; there is, therefore, no such thing contained in them. A little attention will discover to us that the very being of an idea implies passiveness and inertness in it, insomuch that it is im-

---

*The bracketed sentence is omitted from the second edition.

possible for an idea to do anything, or, strictly speaking, to be the cause of anything: neither can it be the resemblance or pattern of any active being, as is evident from sect. 8. Whence it plainly follows that extension, figure, and motion cannot be the cause of our sensations. To say, therefore, that these are the effects of powers resulting from the configuration, number, motion, and size of corpuscles, must certainly be false.

26. We perceive a continual succession of ideas, some are anew excited, others are changed or totally disappear. There is therefore some cause of these ideas, whereon they depend, and which produces and changes them. That this cause cannot be any quality or idea or combination of ideas, is clear from the preceding section. It must therefore be a substance; but it has been shewn that there is no corporeal or material substance: it remains therefore that the cause of ideas is an incorporeal active substance or Spirit.

27. A spirit is one simple, undivided, active being— as it perceives ideas it is called the *understanding,* and as it produces or otherwise operates about them it is called the *will.* Hence there can be no *idea* formed of a soul or spirit; for all ideas whatever, being passive and inert (Vide sect. 25), they cannot represent unto us, by way of image or likeness, that which acts. A little attention will make it plain to any one, that to have an idea which shall be like that active principle of motion and change of ideas is absolutely impossible. Such is the nature of *spirit,* or that which acts, that it cannot be of itself perceived, but only by the effects which it produceth. If any man shall doubt of the truth of what is here delivered, let him but reflect and try if he can frame the idea of any power or active being, and whether he has ideas of two principal powers, marked by

the names *will* and *understanding,* distinct from each other as well as from a third idea of Substance or Being in general, with a relative notion of its supporting or being the subject of the aforesaid powers—which is signified by the name *soul* or *spirit.* This is what some hold; but, so far as I can see, the words *will, soul, spirit,* do not stand for different ideas, or, in truth, for any idea at all, but for something which is very different from ideas, and which, being an agent, cannot be like unto, or represented by, any idea whatsoever. [Though it must be owned at the same time that we have some *notion* of soul, spirit, and the operations of the mind: such as willing, loving, hating—inasmuch as we know or understand the meaning of these words.]*

28. I find I can excite ideas in my mind at pleasure, and vary and shift the scene as oft as I think fit. It is no more than willing, and straightway this or that idea arises in my fancy; and by the same power it is obliterated and makes way for another. This making and unmaking of ideas doth very properly denominate the mind active. Thus much is certain and grounded on experience; but when we think of unthinking agents or of exciting ideas exclusive of volition, we only amuse ourselves with words.

29. But, whatever power I may have over my own thoughts, I find the ideas actually perceived by Sense have not a like dependence on my will. When in broad daylight I open my eyes, it is not in my power to choose whether I shall see or no, or to determine what particular objects shall present themselves to my view; and so likewise as to the hearing and other senses; the ideas imprinted on them are not creatures of my will. There

---

*The bracketed sentence was added to the last edition.

is therefore some *other* Will or Spirit that produces them.

30. The ideas of Sense are more strong, lively, and distinct than those of the imagination; they have likewise a steadiness, order, and coherence, and are not excited at random, as those which are the effects of human wills often are, but in a regular train or series, the admirable connexion whereof sufficiently testifies the wisdom and benevolence of its Author. Now the set rules or established methods wherein the Mind we depend on excites in us the ideas of sense, are called the *laws of nature;* and these we learn by experience, which teaches us that such and such ideas are attended with such and such other ideas, in the ordinary course of things.

31. This gives us a sort of foresight which enables us to regulate our actions for the benefit of life. And without this we should be eternally at a loss; we could not know how to act anything that might procure us the least pleasure, or remove the least pain of sense. That food nourishes, sleep refreshes, and fire warms us; that to sow in the seed-time is the way to reap in the harvest; and in general that to obtain such or such ends, such or such means are conducive—all this we know, not by discovering any necessary connexion between our ideas, but only by the observation of the settled laws of nature, without which we should be all in uncertainty and confusion, and a grown man no more know how to manage himself in the affairs of life than an infant just born.

32. And yet this consistent uniform working, which so evidently displays the goodness and wisdom of that Governing Spirit whose Will constitutes the laws of nature, is so far from leading our thoughts

to Him, that it rather sends them wandering after second causes. For, when we perceive certain ideas of Sense constantly followed by other ideas and we know this is not of our own doing, we forthwith attribute power and agency to the ideas themselves, and make one the cause of another, than which nothing can be more absurd and unintelligible. Thus, for example, having observed that when we perceive by sight a certain round luminous figure we at the same time perceive by touch the idea or sensation called heat, we do from thence conclude the sun to be the cause of heat. And in like manner perceiving the motion and collision of bodies to be attended with sound, we are inclined to think the latter the effect of the former.

33. The ideas imprinted on the Senses by the Author of nature are called *real things;* and those excited in the imagination being less regular, vivid, and constant, are more properly termed *ideas,* or *images of things,* which they copy and represent. But then our sensations, be they never so vivid and distinct, are nevertheless ideas, that is, they exist in the mind, or are perceived by it, as truly as the ideas of its own framing. The ideas of Sense are allowed to have more reality in them, that is, to be more strong, orderly, and coherent than the creatures of the mind; but this is no argument that they exist without the mind. They are also less dependent on the spirit, or thinking substance which perceives them, in that they are excited by the will of another and more powerful spirit; yet still they are *ideas,* and certainly no idea, whether faint or strong, can exist otherwise than in a mind perceiving it.

34. Before we proceed any farther it is necessary we spend some time in answering objections which may

probably be made against the principles we have hitherto laid down. In doing of which, if I seem too prolix to those of quick apprehensions, I hope it may be pardoned, since all men do not equally apprehend things of this nature, and I am willing to be understood by every one.

First, then, it will be objected that by the foregoing principles all that is real and substantial in nature is banished out of the world, and instead thereof a chimerical scheme of *ideas* takes place. All things that exist, exist only in the mind, that is, they are purely notional. What therefore becomes of the sun, moon and stars? What must we think of houses, rivers, mountains, trees, stones; nay, even of our own bodies? Are all these but so many chimeras and illusions on the fancy? To all which, and whatever else of the same sort may be objected, I answer, that by the principles premised we are not deprived of any one thing in nature. Whatever we see, feel, hear, or anywise conceive or understand remains as secure as ever, and is as real as ever. There is a *rerum natura,* and the distinction between realities and chimeras retains its full force. This is evident from sect. 29, 30, and 33, where we have shewn what is meant by *real things* in opposition to *chimeras* or ideas of our own framing; but then they both equally exist in the mind, and in that sense they are alike *ideas.*

35. I do not argue against the existence of any one thing that we can apprehend either by sense or reflexion. That the things I see with my eyes and touch with my hands do exist, really exist, I make not the least question. The only thing whose existence we deny is that which *philosophers* call Matter or corporeal substance. And in doing of this there is no damage done to the

rest of mankind, who, I dare say, will never miss it. The Atheist indeed will want the colour of an empty name to support his impiety; and the Philosophers may possibly find they have lost a great handle for trifling and disputation. [But that is all the harm that I can see done.]*

36. If any man thinks this detracts from the existence or reality of things, he is very far from understanding what hath been premised in the plainest terms I could think of. Take here an abstract of what has been said:—There are spiritual substances, minds, or human souls, which will or excite ideas in themselves at pleasure; but these are faint, weak, and unsteady in respect of others they perceive by sense—which, being impressed upon them according to certain rules or laws of nature, speak themselves the effects of a mind more powerful and wise than human spirits. These latter are said to have more *reality* in them than the former:—by which is meant that they are more affecting, orderly, and distinct, and that they are not fictions of the mind perceiving them. And in this sense the sun that I see by day is the real sun, and that which I imagine by night is the idea of the former. In the sense here given of *reality* it is evident that every vegetable, star, mineral, and in general each part of the mundane system, is as much a *real being* by our principles as by any other. Whether others mean anything by the term *reality* different from what I do, I entreat them to look into their own thoughts and see.

37. It will be urged that thus much at least is true, to wit, that we take away all corporeal substances. To this my answer is, that if the word *substance* be taken

---

*Omitted from second edition.

in the vulgar sense—for a combination of sensible qualities, such as extension, solidity, weight, and the like—this we cannot be accused of taking away: but if it be taken in a philosophic sense—for the support of accidents or qualities without the mind—then indeed I acknowledge that we take it away, if one may be said to take away that which never had any existence, not even in the imagination.

38. But after all, say you, it sounds very harsh to say we eat and drink ideas, and are clothed with ideas. I acknowledge it does so—the word *idea* not being used in common discourse to signify the several combinations of sensible qualities which are called *things;* and it is certain that any expression which varies from the familiar use of language will seem harsh and ridiculous. But this doth not concern the truth of the proposition, which in other words is no more than to say, we are fed and clothed with those things which we perceive immediately by our senses. The hardness or softness, the colour, taste, warmth, figure, or suchlike qualities, which combined together constitute the several sorts of victuals and apparel, have been shewn to exist only in the mind that perceives them; and this is all that is meant by calling them *ideas;* which word if it was as ordinarily used as *thing,* would sound no harsher nor more ridiculous than it. I am not for disputing about the propriety, but the truth of the expression. If therefore you agree with me that we eat and drink and are clad with the immediate objects of sense, which cannot exist unperceived or without the mind, I shall readily grant it is more proper or conformable to custom that they should be called things rather than ideas.

39. If it be demanded why I make use of the word *idea,* and do not rather in compliance with custom call

them *things;* I answer, I do it for two reasons:—first, because the term *thing* in contradistinction to *idea,* is generally supposed to denote somewhat existing without the mind; secondly, because *thing* hath a more comprehensive signification than *idea,* including spirit or thinking things as well as ideas. Since therefore the objects of sense exist only in the mind, and are withal thoughtless and inactive, I chose to mark them by the word *idea,* which implies those properties.

40. But, say what we can, some one perhaps may be apt to reply, he will still believe his senses, and never suffer any arguments, how plausible soever, to prevail over the certainty of them. Be it so; assert the evidence of sense as high as you please, we are willing to do the same. That what I see, hear, and feel doth exist, that is to say, is perceived by me, I no more doubt than I do of my own being. But I do not see how the testimony of sense can be alleged as a proof for the existence of anything which is not perceived by sense. We are not for having any man turn sceptic and disbelieve his senses; on the contrary, we give them all the stress and assurance imaginable; nor are there any principles more opposite to Scepticism than those we have laid down, as shall be hereafter clearly shewn.

41. *Secondly,* it will be objected that there is a great difference betwixt real fire for instance, and the idea of fire, betwixt dreaming or imagining oneself burnt, and actually being so: if you suspect it to be only the idea of fire which you see, do but put your hand into it and you will be convinced with a witness. This and the like may be urged in opposition to our tenets. To all which the answer is evident from what hath been already said; and I shall only add in this place,

that if real fire be very different from the idea of fire, so also is the real pain that it occasions very different from the idea of the same pain, and yet nobody will pretend that real pain either is, or can possibly be, in an unperceiving thing, or without the mind, any more than its idea.

42. *Thirdly,* it will be objected that we see things actually without or at distance from us, and which consequently do not exist in the mind; it being absurd that those things which are seen at the distance of several miles should be as near to us as our own thoughts. In answer to this, I desire it may be considered that in a dream we do oft perceive things as existing at a great distance off, and yet for all that, those things are acknowledged to have their existence only in the mind.

43. But, for the fuller clearing of this point, it may be worth while to consider how it is that we perceive distance and things placed at a distance by sight. For, that we should in truth see external space, and bodies actually existing in it, some nearer, others farther off, seems to carry with it some opposition to what hath been said of their existing nowhere without the mind. The consideration of this difficulty it was that gave birth to my "Essay towards a New Theory of Vision," which was published not long since, wherein it is shewn that distance or outness is neither immediately of itself perceived by sight, nor yet apprehended or judged of by lines and angles, or anything that hath a necessary connexion with it; but that it is only suggested to our thoughts by certain visible ideas and sensations attending vision, which in their own nature have no manner of similitude or relation either with distance or things placed at a distance; but, by a con-

nexion taught us by experience, they come to signify and suggest them to us, after the same manner that words of any language suggest the ideas they are made to stand for; insomuch that a man born blind and afterwards made to see, would not, at first sight, think the things he saw to be without his mind, or at any distance from him. See sect. 41 of the forementioned treatise.

44. The ideas of sight and touch make two species entirely distinct and heterogeneous. The former are marks and prognostics of the latter. That the proper objects of sight neither exist without mind, nor are the images of external things, was shewn even in that treatise. Though throughout the same the contrary be supposed true of tangible objects—not that to suppose that vulgar error was necessary for establishing the notion therein laid down, but because it was beside my purpose to examine and refute it in a discourse concerning *Vision.* So that in strict truth the ideas of sight, when we apprehend by them distance and things placed at a distance, do not suggest or mark out to us things actually existing at a distance, but only admonish us what ideas of touch will be imprinted in our minds at such and such distances of time, and in consequence of such or such actions. It is, I say, evident from what has been said in the foregoing parts of this Treatise, and in sect. 147 and elsewhere of the Essay concerning Vision, that visible ideas are the Language whereby the Governing Spirit on whom we depend informs us what tangible ideas he is about to imprint upon us, in case we excite this or that motion in our own bodies. But for a fuller information in this point I refer to the Essay itself.

45. *Fourthly,* it will be objected that from the fore

going principles it follows things are every moment
annihilated and created anew. The objects of sense exist only when they are perceived; the trees therefore are
in the garden, or the chairs in the parlour, no longer
than while there is somebody by to perceive them.
Upon shutting my eyes all the furniture in the room is
reduced to nothing, and barely upon opening them
it is again created. In answer to all which, I refer
the reader to what has been said in sect. 3, 4, &c., and
desire he will consider whether he means anything by
the actual existence of an idea distinct from its being
perceived. For my part, after the nicest inquiry I
could make, I am not able to discover that anything
else is meant by those words; and I once more entreat
the reader to sound his own thoughts, and not suffer
himself to be imposed on by words. If he can conceive it possible either for his ideas or their archetypes
to exist without being perceived, then I give up the
cause; but if he cannot, he will acknowledge it is un-
reasonable for him to stand up in defence of he knows
not what, and pretend to charge on me as an absurdity
the not assenting to those propositions which at bottom
have no meaning in them.

46. It will not be amiss to observe how far the received principles of philosophy are themselves charge-
able with those pretended absurdities. It is thought
strangely absurd that upon closing my eyelids all the
visible objects around me should be reduced to nothing;
and yet is not this what philosophers commonly acknowledge, when they agree on all hands that light
and colours, which alone are the proper and immediate
objects of sight, are mere sensations that exist no
longer than they are perceived? Again, it may to some
perhaps seem very incredible that things should be

every moment creating, yet this very notion is commonly taught in the schools. For the Schoolmen, though they acknowledge the existence of Matter, and that the whole mundane fabric is framed out of it, are nevertheless of opinion that it cannot subsist without the divine conservation, which by them is expounded to be a continual creation.

47. Farther, a little thought will discover to us that though we allow the existence of Matter or corporeal substance, yet it will unavoidably follow, from the principles which are now generally admitted, that the particular bodies, of what kind soever, do none of them exist whilst they are not perceived. For, it is evident from sect. 11 and the following sections, that the Matter philosophers contend for is an incomprehensible somewhat, which hath none of those particular qualities whereby the bodies falling under our senses are distinguished one from another. But, to make this more plain, it must be remarked that the infinite divisibility of Matter is now universally allowed, at least by the most approved and considerable philosophers, who on the received principles demonstrate it beyond all exception. Hence, it follows there is an infinite number of parts in each particle of Matter which are not perceived by sense. The reason therefore that any particular body seems to be of a finite magnitude, or exhibits only a finite number of parts to sense, is, not because it contains no more, since in itself it contains an infinite number of parts, but because the sense is not acute enough to discern them. In proportion therefore as the sense is rendered more acute, it perceives a greater number of parts in the object, that is, the object appears greater, and its figure varies, those parts in its extremities which were before

unperceivable appearing now to bound it in very different lines and angles from those perceived by an obtuser
sense. And at length, after various changes of size and
shape, when the sense becomes infinitely acute the body
shall seem infinite. During all which there is no alteration in the body, but only in the sense. Each body
therefore, considered in itself, is infinitely extended,
and consequently void of all shape or figure. From
which it follows that, though we should grant the existence of Matter to be never so certain, yet it is withal
as certain, the materialists themselves are by their own
principles forced to acknowledge, that neither the particular bodies perceived by sense, nor anything like
them, exists without the mind. Matter, I say, and each
particle thereof, is according to them infinite and shapeless, and it is the mind that frames all that variety of
bodies which compose the visible world, any one whereof does not exist longer than it is perceived.

48. If we consider it, the objection proposed in sect.
45 will not be found reasonably charged on the principles we have premised, so as in truth to make any objection at all against our notions. For, though we hold
indeed the objects of sense to be nothing else but ideas
which cannot exist unperceived; yet we may not hence
conclude they have no existence except only while they
are perceived by us, since there may be some other
spirit that perceives them though we do not. Wherever
bodies are said to have no existence without the mind,
I would not be understood to mean this or that particular mind, but all minds whatsoever. It does not
therefore follow from the foregoing principles that
bodies are annihilated and created every moment, or
exist not at all during the intervals between our perception of them.

49. *Fifthly,* it may perhaps be objected that if **extension** and figure exist only in the mind, it follows that the mind is extended and figured; since extension is a mode or attribute which (to speak with the schools) is predicated of the subject in which it exists. I answer, those qualities are in the mind only as they are perceived by it—that is, not by way of *mode* or *attribute,* but only by way of *idea;* and it no more follows the soul or mind is extended, because extension exists in it alone, than it does that it is red or blue, because those colours are on all hands acknowledged to exist in it, and nowhere else. As to what philosophers say of subject and mode, that seems very groundless and unintelligible. For instance, in this proposition "a die is hard, extended, and square," they will have it that the word *die* denotes a subject or substance, distinct from the hardness, extension, and figure which are predicated of it, and in which they exist. This I cannot comprehend: to me a die seems to be nothing distinct from those things which are termed its modes or accidents. And, to say a die is hard, extended, and square is not to attribute those qualities to a subject distinct from and nowhere else. As to what philosophers say of meaning of the word *die.*

50. *Sixthly,* you will say there have been a great many things explained by matter and motion; take away these and you destroy the whole corpuscular philosophy, and undermine those mechanical principles which have been applied with so much success to account for the phenomena. In short, whatever advances have been made, either by ancient or modern philosophers, in the study of nature do all proceed on the supposition that corporeal substance or Matter doth really

exist. To this I answer that there is not any one phenomenon explained on that supposition which may not
as well be explained without it, as might easily be made
appear by an induction of particulars. To explain the
phenomena, is all one as to shew why, upon such and
such occasions, we are affected with such and such
ideas. But how Matter should operate on a Spirit, or
produce any idea in it, is what no philosopher will pretend to explain; it is therefore evident there can be no
use of Matter in natural philosophy. Besides, they
who attempt to account for things do it not by corporeal
substance, but by figure, motion, and other qualities,
which are in truth no more than mere ideas, and, therefore, cannot be the cause of anything, as hath been
already shewn. See sect. 25.

51. *Seventhly,* it will upon this be demanded whether
it does not seem absurd to take away natural causes,
and ascribe everything to the immediate operation of
Spirits? We must no longer say upon these principles
that fire heats, or water cools, but that a Spirit heats,
and so forth. Would not a man be deservedly laughed
at, who should talk after this manner? I answer, he
would so; in such things we ought to "think with the
learned, and speak with the vulgar." They who to
demonstration are convinced of the truth of the Coper-
nican system do nevertheless say "the sun rises," "the
sun sets," or "comes to the meridian;" and if they
affected a contrary style in common talk it would without doubt appear very ridiculous. A little reflexion on
what is here said will make it manifest that the common
use of language would receive no manner of alteration
or disturbance from the admission of our tenets.

52. In the ordinary affairs of life, any phrases may

be retained, so long as they excite in us proper senti-
ments, or dispositions to act in such a manner as is
necessary for our well-being, how false soever they
may be if taken in a strict and speculative sense. Nay,
this is unavoidable, since, propriety being regulated
by custom, language is suited to the received opinions,
which are not always the truest. Hence it is impossible, even in the most rigid, philosophic reasonings, so
far to alter the bent and genius of the tongue we speak,
as never to give a handle for cavillers to pretend difficulties and inconsistencies. But, a fair and ingenuous
reader will collect the sense from the scope and tenor
and connexion of a discourse, making allowances for
those inaccurate modes of speech which use has made
inevitable.

53. As to the opinion that there are no Corporeal
Causes, this has been heretofore maintained by some
of the Schoolmen, as it is of late by others among the
modern philosophers, who though they allow Matter
to exist, yet will have God alone to be the immediate
efficient cause of all things. These men saw that
amongst all the objects of sense there was none which
had any power or activity included in it; and that by
consequence this was likewise true of whatever bodies
they supposed to exist without the mind, like unto the
immediate objects of sense. But then, that they should
suppose an innumerable multitude of created beings,
which they acknowledge are not capable of producing
any one effect in nature, and which therefore are made
to no manner of purpose, since God might have done
everything as well without them: this I say, though
we should allow it possible, must yet be a very unaccountable and extravagant supposition.

54. In the *eighth* place, the universal concurrent

assent of mankind may be thought by some an invincible argument in behalf of Matter, or the existence of external things.   Must we suppose the whole world to be mistaken?   And if so, what cause can be assigned of so widespread and predominant an error?   I answer, first, that, upon a narrow inquiry, it will not perhaps be found so many as is imagined do really believe the existence of Matter or things without the mind. Strictly speaking, to believe that which involves a contradiction, or has no meaning in it, is impossible; and whether the foregoing expressions are not of that sort, I refer it to the impartial examination of the reader. In one sense, indeed, men may be said to believe that Matter exists, that is, they act as if the immediate cause of their sensations, which affects them every moment, and is so nearly present to them, were some senseless unthinking being.   But, that they should clearly apprehend any meaning marked by those words, and form thereof a settled speculative opinion, is what I am not able to conceive.   This is not the only instance wherein men impose upon themselves, by imagining they believe those propositions which they have often heard, though at bottom they have no meaning in them.

55. But secondly, though we should grant a notion to be never so universally and steadfastly adhered to, yet this is weak argument of its truth to whoever considers what a vast number of prejudices and false opinions are everywhere embraced with the utmost tenaciousness, by the unreflecting (which are the far greater) part of mankind.   There was a time when the antipodes and motion of the earth were looked upon as monstrous absurdities even by men of learning: and if it be considered what a small proportion they bear

to the rest of mankind, we shall find that at this day those notions have gained but a very inconsiderable footing in the world.

56. But it is demanded that we assign a cause of this prejudice, and account for its obtaining in the world. To this I answer, that men knowing they perceived several ideas, whereof they themselves were not the authors—as not being excited from within nor depending on the operation of their wills—this made them maintain those ideas, or objects of perception had an existence independent of and without the mind, without ever dreaming that a contradiction was involved in those words. But, philosophers having plainly seen that the immediate objects of perception do not exist without the mind, they in some degree corrected the mistake of the vulgar; but at the same time run into another which seems no less absurd, to wit, that there are certain objects really existing without the mind, or having a subsistence distinct from being perceived, of which our ideas are only images or resemblances, imprinted by those objects on the mind. And this notion of the philosophers owes its origin to the same cause with the former, namely, their being conscious that they were not the authors of their own sensations, which they evidently knew were imprinted from without, and which therefore must have some cause distinct from the minds on which they are imprinted.

57. But why they should suppose the ideas of sense to be excited in us by things in their likeness, and not rather have recourse to *Spirit* which alone can act, may be accounted for, first, because they were not aware of the repugnancy there is, as well in supposing things

like unto our ideas existing without, as in attributing to them power or activity. Secondly, because the Supreme Spirit which excites those ideas in our minds, is not marked out and limited to our view by any particular finite collection of sensible ideas, as human agents are by their size, complexion, limbs, and motions. And thirdly, because His operations are regular and uniform. Whenever the course of nature is interrupted by a miracle, men are ready to own the presence of a superior agent. But, when we see things go on in the ordinary course they do not excite in us any reflexion; their order and concatenation, though it be an argument of the greatest wisdom, power, and goodness in their creator, is yet so constant and familiar to us that we do not think them the immediate effects of a *Free Spirit;* especially since inconsistency and mutability in acting, though it be an imperfection, is looked on as a mark of *freedom.*

58. *Tenthly,* it will be objected that the notions we advance are inconsistent with several sound truths in philosophy and mathematics. For example, the motion of the earth is now universally admitted by astronomers as a truth grounded on the clearest and most convincing reasons. But, on the foregoing principles, there can be no such thing. For, motion being only an idea, it follows that if it be not perceived it exists not; but the motion of the earth is not perceived by sense. I answer, that tenet, if rightly understood, will be found to agree with the principles we have premised; for, the question whether the earth moves or no amounts in reality to no more than this, to wit, whether we have reason to conclude, from what has been observed by astronomers, that if we were placed

in such and such circumstances, and such or such a position and distance both from the earth and sun, we should perceive the former to move among the choir of the planets, and appearing in all respects like one of them; and this, by the established rules of nature which we have no reason to mistrust, is reasonably collected from the phenomena.

59. We may, from the experience we have had of the train and succession of ideas in our minds, often make, I will not say uncertain conjectures, but sure and well-grounded predictions concerning the ideas we shall be affected with pursuant to a great train of actions, and be enabled to pass a right judgment of what would have appeared to us, in case we were placed in circumstances very different from those we are in at present. Herein consists the knowledge of nature, which may preserve its use and certainty very consistently with what hath been said. It will be easy to apply this to whatever objections of the like sort may be drawn from the magnitude of the stars, or any other discoveries in astronomy or nature.

60. In the *eleventh* place, it will be demanded to what purpose serves that curious organization of plants, and the animal mechanism in the parts of animals; might not vegetables grow, and shoot forth leaves of blossoms, and animals perform all their motions as well without as with all that variety of internal parts so elegantly contrived and put together; which, being ideas, have nothing powerful or operative in them, nor have any necessary connexion with the effects ascribed to them? If it be a Spirit that immediately produces every effect by a *fiat* or act of his will, we must think all that is fine and artificial in the works,

whether of man or nature, to be made in vain. By this doctrine, though an artist hath made the spring and wheels, and every movement of a watch, and adjusted them in such a manner as he knew would produce the motions he designed, yet he must think all this done to no purpose, and that it is an Intelligence which directs the index, and points to the hour of the day. If so, why may not the Intelligence do it, without his being at the pains of making the movements and putting them together? Why does not an empty case serve as well as another? And how comes it to pass that whenever there is any fault in the going of a watch, there is some corresponding disorder to be found in the movements, which being mended by a skilful hand all is right again? The like may be said of all the clockwork of nature, great part whereof is so wonderfully fine and subtle as scarce to be discerned by the best microscope. In short, it will be asked, how, upon our principles, any tolerable account can be given, or any final cause assigned of an innumerable multitude of bodies and machines, framed with the most exquisite art, which in the common philosophy have very apposite uses assigned them, and serve to explain abundance of phenomena?

61. To all which I answer, first, that though there were some difficulties relating to the administration of Providence, and the uses by it assigned to the several parts of nature, which I could not solve by the foregoing principles, yet this objection could be of small weight against the truth and certainty of those things which may be proved *a priori*, with the utmost evidence and rigor of demonstration. Secondly, but neither are the received principles free from the like difficulties; for, it may still be demanded to what end

God should take those roundabout methods of effecting things by instruments and machines, which no one can deny might have been effected by the mere command of His will without all that apparatus; nay, if we narrowly consider it, we shall find the objection may be retorted with greater force on those who hold the existence of those machines without of mind; for it has been made evident that solidity, bulk, figure, motion, and the like have no *activity* or *efficacy* in them, so as to be capable of producing any one effect in nature. See sect. 25. Whoever therefore supposes them to exist (allowing the supposition possible) when they are not perceived does it manifestly to no purpose; since the only use that is assigned to them, as they exist unperceived, is that they produce those perceivable effects which in truth cannot be ascribed to anything but Spirit.

62. But, to come nigher the difficulty, it must be observed that though the fabrication of all those parts and organs be not absolutely necessary to the producing any effect, yet it is necessary to the producing of things in a constant regular way according to the laws of nature. There are certain general laws that run through the whole chain of natural effects; these are learned by the observation and study of nature, and are by men applied as well to the framing artificial things for the use and ornament of life as to the explaining various phenomena—which explication consists only in shewing the conformity any particular phenomenon hath to the general laws of nature, or, which is the same thing, in discovering the *uniformity* there is in the production of natural effects; as will be evident to whoever shall attend to the several instances wherein philosophers pretend to account for appearances. That

there is a great and conspicuous use in these regular constant methods of working observed by the Supreme Agent hath been shewn in sect. 31. And it is no less visible that a particular size, figure, motion, and disposition of parts are necessary, though not absolutely to the producing any effect, yet to the producing it according to the standing mechanical laws of nature. Thus, for instance, it cannot be denied that God, or the Intelligence that sustains and rules the ordinary course of things, might if He were minded to produce a miracle, cause all the motions on the dial-plate of a watch, though nobody had ever made the movements and put them in it: but yet, if He will act agreeably to the rules of mechanism, by Him for wise ends established and maintained in the creation, it is necessary that those actions of the watchmaker, whereby he makes the movements and rightly adjusts them, precede the production of the aforesaid motions; as also that any disorder in them be attended with the perception of some corresponding disorder in the movements, which being once corrected all is right again.

63. It may indeed on some occasions be necessary that the Author of nature display His overruling power in producing some appearance out of the ordinary series of things. Such exceptions from the general rules of nature are proper to surprise and awe men into an acknowledgement of the Divine Being; but then they are to be used but seldom, otherwise there is a plain reason why they should fail of that effect. Besides, God seems to choose the convincing our reason of His attributes by the works of nature, which discover so much harmony and contrivance in their make, and are such plain indications of

wisdom and beneficence in their Author, rather than to astonish us into a belief of His Being by anomalous and surprising events.

64. To set this matter in a yet clearer light, I shall observe that what has been objected in sect. 60 amounts in reality to no more than this :—ideas are not anyhow and at random produced, there being a certain order and connexion between them, like to that of cause and effect; there are also several combinations of them made in a very regular and artificial manner, which seem like so many instruments in the hand of nature that, being hid as it were behind the scenes, have a secret operation in producing those appearances which are seen on the theatre of the world, being themselves discernible only to the curious eye of the philosopher. But, since one idea cannot be the cause of another, to what purpose is that connexion? And, since those instruments, being barely *inefficacious perceptions* in the mind, are not subservient to the production of natural effects, it is demanded why they are made; or, in other words, what reason can be assigned why God should make us, upon a close inspection into His works, behold so great variety of ideas so artfully laid together, and so much according to rule; it not being [credible]* that He would be at the expense (if one may so speak) of all that art and regularity to no purpose.

65. To all which my answer is, first, that the connexion of ideas does not imply the relation of *cause* and *effect,* but only of a mark or *sign* with the thing *signified.* The fire which I see is not the cause of the pain I suffer upon my approaching it, but the mark that forewarns me of it. In like manner the noise that

---

*"Imaginable" in the first edition.

I hear is not the effect of this or that motion or collision of the ambient bodies, but the sign thereof. Secondly, the reason why ideas are formed into machines, that is, artificial and regular combinations, is the same with that for combining letters into words. That a few original ideas may be made to signify a great number of effects and actions, it is necessary they be variously combined together. And, to the end their use be permanent and universal, these combinations must be made by *rule,* and with *wise contrivance.* By this means abundance of information is conveyed unto us, concerning what we are to expect from such and such actions and what methods are proper to be taken for the exciting such and such ideas; which in effect is all that I conceive to be distinctly meant when it is said that, by discerning a figure, texture, and mechanism of the inward parts of bodies, whether natural or artificial, we may attain to know the several uses and properties depending thereon, or the nature of the thing.

66. Hence, it is evident that those things which, under the notion of a cause co-operating or concurring to the production of effects, are altogether inexplicable, and run us into great absurdities, may be very naturally explained, and have a proper and obvious use assigned to them, when they are considered only as marks or signs for our information. And it is the searching after and endeavouring to understand [those signs instituted by the Author of Nature]*, that ought to be the employment of the natural philosopher; and not the pretending to explain things by corporeal causes, which doctrine seems to have too much es-

---

*In the first edition the bracketed phrase reads as follows: "this Language (if I may so call it) of the Author of Nature."

tranged the minds of men from that active principle, that supreme and wise Spirit "in whom we live, move, and have our being."

67. In the *twelfth* place, it may perhaps be objected that—though it be clear from what has been said that there can be no such thing as an inert, senseless, extended, solid, figured, movable substance existing without the mind, such as philosophers describe Matter—yet, if any man shall leave out of his idea of *matter* the positive ideas of extension, figure, solidity and motion, and say that he means only by that word an inert, senseless substance, that exists without the mind or unperceived, which is the occasion of our ideas, or at the presence whereof God is pleased to excite ideas in us: it doth not appear but that Matter taken in this sense may possibly exist. In answer to which I say, first, that it seems no less absurd to suppose a substance without accidents, than it is to suppose accidents without a substance. But secondly, though we should grant this unknown substance may possibly exist, yet where can it be supposed to be? That it exists not in the mind is agreed; and that it exists not in place is no less certain—since all place or extension exists only in the mind, as hath been already proved. It remains therefore that it exists nowhere at all.

68. Let us examine a little the description that is here given us of *matter*. It neither acts, nor perceives, nor is perceived; for this is all that is meant by saying it is an inert, senseless, unknown substance; which is a definition entirely made up of negatives, excepting only the relative notion of its standing under or supporting. But then it must be observed that it supports nothing at all, and how nearly this comes to the de-

scription of a *nonentity* I desire may be considered. But, say you, it is the *unknown occasion,* at the presence of which ideas are excited in us by the will of God. Now, I would fain know how anything can be present to us, which is neither perceivable by sense nor reflexion, nor capable of producing any idea in our minds, nor is at all extended, nor hath any form, nor exists in any place. The words "to be present," when thus applied, must needs be taken in some abstract and strange meaning, and which I am not able to comprehend.

69. Again, let us examine what is meant by *occasion.* So far as I can gather from the common use of language, that word signifies either the agent which produces any effect, or else something that is observed to accompany or go before it in the ordinary course of things. But when it is applied to Matter as above described, it can be taken in neither of those senses; for Matter is said to be passive and inert, and so cannot be an agent or efficient cause. It is also unperceivable, as being devoid of all sensible qualities, and so cannot be the occasion of our perceptions in the latter sense: as when the burning my finger is said to be the occasion of the pain that attends it. What therefore can be meant by calling matter an *occasion?* The term is either used in no sense at all, or else in some very distant from its received signification.

70. You will perhaps say that Matter, though it be not perceived by us, is nevertheless perceived by God, to whom it is the occasion of exciting ideas in our minds. For, say you, since we observe our sensations to be imprinted in an orderly and constant manner, it is but reasonable to suppose there are certain constant and regular occasions of their being produced. That is

to say, that there are certain permanent and distinct parcels of Matter, corresponding to our ideas, which, though they do not excite them in our minds, or any-wise immediately affect us, as being altogether passive and unperceivable to us, they are nevertheless to God, by whom they art perceived, as it were so many occasions to remind Him when and what ideas to imprint on our minds; that so things may go on in a constant uniform manner.

71. In answer to this, I observe that, as the notion of Matter is here stated, the question is no longer concerning the existence of a thing distinct from *Spirit* and *idea,* from perceiving and being perceived; but whether there are not certain ideas of I know not what sort, in the mind of God which are so many marks or notes that direct Him how to produce sensations in our minds in a constant and regular method—much after the same manner as a musician is directed by the notes of music to produce that harmonious train and composition of sound which is called a tune, though they who hear the music do not perceive the notes, and may be entirely ignorant of them. But, this notion of Matter [which after all is the only intelligible one that I can pick, from what is said of unknown occasions]* seems too extravagant to deserve a confutation. Besides, it is in effect no objection against what we have advanced, viz. that there is no senseless unperceived substance.

72. If we follow the light of reason, we shall, from the constant uniform method of our sensations, collect the goodness and wisdom of the Spirit who excites

---

*The bracketed sentence in parentheses was omitted in the second edition.

them in our minds; but this is all that I can see reasonably concluded from thence. To me, I say, it is evident that the being of a spirit infinitely wise, good, and powerful is abundantly sufficient to explain all the appearances of nature. But, as for *inert, senseless Matter,* nothing that I perceive has any the least connexion with it, or leads to the thoughts of it. And I would fain see any one explain any the meanest phenomenon in nature by it, or shew any manner of reason, though in the lowest rank of probability, that he can have for its existence, or even make any tolerable sense or meaning of that supposition. For, as to its being an occasion, we have, I think, evidently shewn that with regard to us it is no occasion. It remains therefore that it must be, if at all, the occasion to God of exciting ideas in us; and what this amounts to we have just now seen.

73. It is worth while to reflect a little on the motives which induced men to suppose the existence of *material substance;* that so having observed the gradual ceasing and expiration of those motives or reasons, we may proportionably withdraw the assent that was grounded on them. First, therefore, it was thought that colour, figure, motion, and the rest of the sensible qualities or accidents, did really exist without the mind; and for this reason it seemed needful to suppose some unthinking *substratum* or substance wherein they did exist, since they could not be conceived to exist by themselves. Afterwards, in process of time, men being convinced that colours, sounds, and the rest of the sensible, secondary qualities had no existence without the mind, they stripped this *substratum* or material substance of those qualities, leaving only the primary ones, figure, motion, and suchlike, which they

still conceived to exist without the mind, and consequently to stand in need of a material support. But, it having been shewn that none even of these can possibly exist otherwise than in a Spirit or Mind which perceives them it follows that we have no longer any reason to suppose the being of Matter; nay, that it is utterly impossible there should be any such thing, so long as that word is taken to denote an *unthinking substratum* of qualities or accidents wherein they exist without the mind.

74. But though it be allowed by the materialists themselves that Matter was thought of only for the sake of supporting accidents, and, the reason entirely ceasing, one might expect the mind should naturally, and without any reluctance at all, quit the belief of what was solely grounded thereon; yet the prejudice is riveted so deeply in our thoughts, that we can scarce tell how to part with it, and are therefore inclined, since the *thing* itself is indefensible, at least to retain the *name,* which we apply to I know not what abstracted and indefinite notions of being, or occasion, though without any show of reason, at least so far as I can see. For, what is there on our part, or what do we perceive, amongst all the ideas, sensations, notions which are imprinted on our minds, either by sense or reflexion, from whence may be inferred the existence of an inert, thoughtless, unperceived occasion? and, on the other hand, on the part of an All-sufficient Spirit, what can there be that should make us believe or even suspect He is directed by an inert occasion to excite ideas in our minds?

75. It is a very extraordinary instance of the force of prejudice, and much to be lamented, that the mind of man retains so great a fondness, against all the

evidence of reason, for a stupid thoughtless *somewhat*, by the interposition whereof it would as it were screen itself from the Providence of God, and remove it farther off from the affairs of the world. But, though we do the utmost we can to secure the belief of Matter, though, when reason forsakes us, we endeavour to support our opinion on the bare possibility of the thing, and though we indulge ourselves in the full scope of an imagination not regulated by reason to make out that poor possibility, yet the upshot of all is, that there are certain *unknown Ideas* in the mind of God; for this, if anything, is all that I conceive to be meant by *occasion* with regard to God. And this at the bottom is no longer contending for the thing, but for the name.

76. Whether therefore there are such Ideas in the mind of God, and whether they may be called by the name *Matter,* I shall not dispute. But, if you stick to the notion of an unthinking substance or support of extension, motion, and other sensible qualities, then to me it is most evidently impossible there should be any such thing; since it is a plain repugnancy that those qualities should exist in or be supported by an unperceiving substance.

77. But, say you, though it be granted that there is no thoughtless support of extension and the other qualities or accidents which we perceive, yet there may perhaps be some inert, unperceiving substance or *substratum* of some other qualities, as incomprehensible to us as colours are to a man born blind, because we have not a sense adapted to them. But, if we had a new sense, we should possibly no more doubt of their existence than a blind man made to see does of the existence of light and colours. I answer, first, if what you mean by the word *Matter* be only the unknown support

of unknown qualities, it is no matter whether there is such a thing or no, since it no way concerns us; and I do not see the advantage there is in disputing about what we know not *what*, and we know not *why*.

78. But, secondly, if we had a new sense it could only furnish us with new ideas or sensations; and then we should have the same reason against their existing in an unperceiving substance that has been already offered with relation to figure, motion, colour, and the like. Qualities, as hath been shewn, are nothing else but *sensations* or *ideas*, which exist only in a *mind* perceiving them; and this is true not only of the ideas we are acquainted with at present, but likewise of all possible ideas whatsoever.

79 But, you will insist, what if I have no reason to believe the existence of Matter? what if I cannot assign any use to it or explain anything by it, or even conceive what is meant by that word? yet still it is no contradiction to say that Matter exists, and that this Matter is in general a *substance*, or *occasion of ideas;* though indeed to go about to unfold the meaning or adhere to any particular explication of those words may be attended with great difficulties. I answer, when words are used without a meaning, you may put them together as you please without danger of running into a contradiction. You may say, for example, that twice two is equal to seven, so long as you declare you do not take the words of that proposition in their usual acceptation but for marks of you know not what. And, by the same reason, you may say there is an inert thoughtless substance without accidents which is the occasion of our ideas. And we shall understand just as much by one proposition as the other.

80. In the *last* place, you will say, what if we give
up the cause of material Substance, and stand to it
that Matter is an unknown *somewhat*—neither substance nor accident, spirit nor idea, inert, thoughtless,
indivisible, immovable, unextended, existing in no
place. For, say you, whatever may be urged against
substance or *occasion,* or any other positive or relative
notion of Matter, hath no place at all, so long as this
negative definition of Matter is adhered to. I answer,
you may, if so it shall seem good, use the word
"Matter" in the same sense as other men use "nothing,"
and so make those terms convertible in your style.
For, after all, this is what appears to me to be the
result of that definition, the parts whereof when I
consider with attention, either collectively or separate
from each other, I do not find that there is any kind of
effect or impression made on my mind different from
what is excited by the term *nothing.*

81. You will reply, perhaps, that in the foresaid
definition is included what doth sufficiently distinguish
it from nothing—the positive abstract idea of *quiddity,
entity*, or *existence.* I own, indeed, that those who pretend to the faculty of framing abstract general ideas
do talk as if they had such an idea, which is, say they,
the most abstract and general notion of all; that is, to
me, the most incomprehensible of all others. That
there are a great variety of spirits of different orders
and capacities, whose faculties both in number and extent are far exceeding those the Author of my being has
bestowed on me, I see no reason to deny. And for me
to pretend to determine by my own few, stinted
narrow inlets of perception, what ideas the inexhausti-
ble power of the Supreme Spirit may imprint upon
them were certainly the utmost folly and presumption

—since there may be, for aught that I know, innumerable sorts of ideas or sensations, as different from one another, and from all that I have perceived, as colours are from sounds. But, how ready soever I may be to acknowledge the scantiness of my comprehension with regard to the endless variety of spirits and ideas that may possibly exist, yet for any one to pretend to a notion of Entity or Existence, *abstracted* from *spirit* and *idea,* from perceived and being perceived, is, I suspect, a downright repugnancy and trifling with words.— It remains that we consider the objections which may possibly be made on the part of Religion.

82. Some there are who think that, though the arguments for the real existence of bodies which are drawn from Reason be allowed not to amount to demonstration, yet the Holy Scriptures are so clear in the point as will sufficiently convince every good Christian that bodies do really exist, and are something more than mere ideas; there being in Holy Writ innumerable facts related which evidently suppose the reality of timber and stone, mountains and rivers, and cities, and human bodies. To which I answer that no sort of writings whatever, sacred or profane, which use those and the like words in the vulgar acceptation, or so as to have a meaning in them, are in danger of having their truth called in question by our doctrine. That all those things do really exist, that there are bodies, even corporeal substances, when taken in the vulgar sense, has been shewn to be agreeable to our principles; and the difference betwixt *things* and *ideas, realities* and *chimeras,* has been distinctly explained. See sec. 29, 30, 33, 36, &c. And I do not think that either what

philosophers call *Matter*, or the existence of objects without the mind, is anywhere mentioned in Scripture.

83. Again, whether there can be or be not external things, it is agreed on all hands that the proper use of words is the marking our conceptions, or things only as they are known and perceived by us; whence it plainly follows that in the tenets we have laid down there is nothing inconsistent with the right use and significancy of language, and that discourse, of what kind soever, so far as it is intelligible, remains undisturbed. But all this seems so manifest, from what has been largely set forth in the premises, that it is needless to insist any farther on it.

84. But, it will be urged that miracles do, at least, lose much of their stress and import by our principles. What must we think of Moses' rod? was it not *really* turned into a serpent; or was there only a change of *ideas* in the minds of the spectators? And, can it be supposed that our Saviour did no more at the marriage-feast in Cana than impose on the sight, and smell, and taste of the guests, so as to create in them the appearance or idea only of wine? The same may be said of all other miracles; which, in consequence of the foregoing principles, must be looked upon only as so many cheats, or illusions of fancy. To this I reply, that the rod was changed into a real serpent, and the water into real wine. That this does not in the least contradict what I have elsewhere said will be evident from sect. 34 and 35. But this business of *real* and *imaginary* has been already so plainly and fully explained, and so often referred to, and the difficulties about it are so easily answered from what has gone before, that it were an affront to the reader's understanding to resume the explication of it in its place. I shall only

observe that if at table all who were present should see, and smell, and taste, and drink wine, and find the effects of it, with me there could be no doubt of its reality; so that at bottom the scruple concerning real miracles has no place at all on ours, but only on the received principles, and consequently makes rather for than against what has been said.

85. Having done with the Objections, which I endeavoured to propose in the clearest light, and gave them all the force and weight I could, we proceed in the next place to take a view of our tenets in their Consequences. Some of these appear at first sight— as that several difficult and obscure questions, on which abundance of speculation has been thrown away, are entirely banished from philosophy. "Whether corporeal substance can think," "whether Matter be infinitely divisible," and "how it operates on spirit"— these and like inquiries have given infinite amusement to philosophers in all ages; but, depending on the existence of Matter, they have no longer any place on our principles. Many other advantages there are, as well with regard to religion as the sciences, which it is easy for any one to deduce from what has been premised; but this will appear more plainly in the sequel.

86. From the principles we have laid down it follows human knowledge may naturally be reduced to two heads—that of *ideas* and that of *spirits*. Of each of these I shall treat in order.

And *first* as to ideas or unthinking things. Our knowledge of these hath been very much obscured and confounded, and we have been led into very dangerous errors, by supposing a twofold existence of the objects of sense—the one *intelligible* or in the mind, the other *real* and without the mind; whereby unthinking things are thought to have a natural subsistence of their own distinct from being perceived by spirits. This, which, if I mistake not, hath been shewn to be a most groundless and absurd notion, is the very root of Scepticism; for, so long as men thought that real things subsisted without the mind, and that their knowledge was only so far forth *real* as it was conformable to *real things,* it follows they could not be certain they had any real knowledge at all. For how can it be known that the things which are perceived are conformable to those which are not perceived, or exist without the mind?

87. Colour, figure, motion, extension, and the like, considered only as so many *sensations* in the mind, are perfectly known, there being nothing in them which is not perceived. But, if they are looked on as notes or images, referred to *things* or *archetypes* existing without the mind, then are we involved all in scepticism. We see only the appearances, and not the real qualities of things. What may be the extension, figure, or motion of anything really and absolutely, or in itself, it is impossible for us to know, but only the proportion or relation they bear to our senses. Things remaining the same, our ideas vary, and which of them, or even whether any of them at all, represent the true quality really existing in the thing, it is out of our reach to determine. So that, for aught we know, all we see, hear, and feel may be only phantom and vain chimera, and not at all agree with the real things existing in *rerum natura.* All this scepticism* follows from our supposing a difference between *things* and *ideas,* and that the former have a subsistence without the mind or

---

* "Sceptical cant" were the words used in the first edition.

unperceived. It were easy to dilate on this subject, and show how the arguments urged by sceptics in all ages depend on the supposition of external objects. [But this is too obvious to need being insisted upon.]*

88. So long as we attribute a real existence to unthinking things, distinct from their being perceived, it is not only impossible for us to know with evidence the nature of any real unthinking being, but even that it exists. Hence it is that we see philosophers distrust their senses, and doubt of the existence of heaven and earth, of everything they see or feel, even of their own bodies. And, after all their labour and struggle of thought, they are forced to own we cannot attain to any self-evident or demonstrative knowledge of the existence of sensible things. But, all this doubtfulness, which so bewilders and confounds the mind and makes philosophy ridiculous in the eyes of the world, vanishes if we annex a meaning to our words, and not amuse ourselves with the terms "absolute," "external," "exist," and such like, signifying we know not what. I can as well doubt of my own being as of the being of those things which I actually perceive by sense; it being a manifest contradiction that any sensible object should be immediately perceived by sight or touch, and at the same time have no existence in nature, since the very *existence* of an unthinking being consists in *being perceived*.

89. Nothing seems of more importance towards erecting a firm system of sound and real knowledge, which may be proof against the assaults of Scepticism, than to lay the beginning in a distinct explication of what is meant by *thing, reality, existence;* for in vain

---

* Omitted in second edition.

shall we dispute concerning the real existence of things, or pretend to any knowledge thereof, so long as we have not fixed the meaning of those words. *Thing* or *Being* is the most general name of all; it comprehends under it two kinds entirely distinct and heterogeneous, and which have nothing common but the name, viz. *spirits* and *ideas.* The former are active, indivisible substances: the latter are inert, fleeting, dependent beings, which subsist not by themselves, but are supported by, or exist in minds or spiritual substances.* We comprehend our own existence by inward feeling or reflexion, and that of other spirits by reason. We may be said to have some knowledge or notion of our own minds, of spirits and active beings, whereof in a strict sense we have not ideas. In like manner, we know and have a notion of relations between things or ideas—which relations are distinct from the ideas or things related, inasmuch as the latter may be perceived by us without our perceiving the former. To me it seems that *ideas, spirits,* and *relations* are all in their respective kinds the object of human knowledge and subject of discourse; and that the term *idea* would be improperly extended to signify everything we know or have any notion of.

90. Ideas imprinted on the senses are real things, or do really exist; this we do not deny, but we deny they can subsist without the minds which perceive them, or that they are resemblances of any archetypes existing without the mind; since the very being of a

---

*In the first edition section 89 ended at this point, and its concluding sentence instead of as it here stands read as follows: "The former are *active, indivisible, incorruptible,* substances: the latter are *inert, fleeting, perishable passions* or *dependent beings* . . . spiritual substances."

sensation or idea consists in being perceived, and an idea can be like nothing but an idea. Again, the things perceived by sense may be termed *external,* with regard to their origin—in that they are not generated from within by the mind itself, but imprinted by a Spirit distinct from that which perceives them. Sensible objects may likewise be said to be "without the mind" in another sense, namely when they exist in some other mind; thus, when I shut my eyes, the things I saw may still exist, but it must be in another mind.

91. It were a mistake to think that what is here said derogates in the least from the reality of things. It is acknowledged, on the received principles, that extension, motion, and in a word all sensible qualities have need of a support, as not being able to subsist by themselves. But the objects perceived by sense are allowed to be nothing but combinations of those qualities, and consequently cannot subsist by themselves. Thus far it is agreed on all hand. So that in denying the things perceived by sense an existence independent of a substance of support wherein they may exist, we detract nothing from the received opinion of their *reality,* and are guilty of no innovation in that respect. All the difference is that, according to us, the unthinking beings perceived by sense have no existence distinct from being perceived, and cannot therefore exist in any other substance than those unextended indivisible substances or *spirits* which act and think and perceive them; whereas philosophers vulgarly hold that the sensible qualities do exist in an inert, extended, unperceiving substance which they call *Matter,* to which they attribute a natural subsistence, exterior to all thinking beings, or distinct from being perceived by any mind whatsoever, even the eternal mind of the Creator,

wherein they suppose only ideas of the corporeal substances created by him; if indeed they allow them to be at all created.

92. For, as we have shewn the doctrine of Matter or corporeal substance to have been the main pillar and support of Scepticism, so likewise upon the same foundation have been raised all the impious schemes of Atheism and Irreligion. Nay, so great a difficulty has it been thought to conceive Matter produced out of nothing, that the most celebrated among the ancient philosophers, even of those who maintained the being of a God, have thought Matter to be uncreated and coeternal with Him. How great a friend *material substance* has been to Atheists in all ages were needless to relate. All their monstrous systems have so visible and necessary a dependence on it that, when this corner-stone is once removed, the whole fabric cannot choose but fall to the ground, insomuch that it is no longer worth while to bestow a particular consideration on the absurdities of every wretched sect of Atheists.

93. That impious and profane persons should readily fall in with those systems which favour their inclinations, by deriding immaterial substance, and supposing the soul to be divisible and subject to corruption as the body; which exclude all freedom, intelligence, and design from the formation of things, and instead thereof make a self-existent, stupid, unthinking substance the root and origin of all beings; that they should hearken to those who deny a Providence, or inspection of a Superior Mind over the affairs of the world, attributing the whole series of events either to blind chance or fatal necessity arising from the impulse of one body or another—all this is very natural. And,

on the other hand, when men of better principles observe the enemies of religion lay so great a stress on
unthinking Matter, and all of them use so much industry and artifice to reduce everything to it, methinks
they should rejoice to see them deprived of their grand
support, and driven from that only fortress, without
which your Epicureans, Hobbists, and the like, have
not even the shadow of a pretence, but become the most
cheap and easy triumph in the world.

94. The existence of Matter, or bodies unperceived,
has not only been the main support of Atheists and
Fatalists, but on the same principle doth Idolatry likewise in all its various forms depend. Did men but
consider that the sun, moon, and stars, and every other
object of the senses are only so many sensations in
their minds, which have no other existence but barely
being perceived, doubtless they would never fall down
and worship their own *ideas,* but rather address their
homage to that ETERNAL INVISIBLE MIND which produces and sustains all things.

95. The same absurd principle, by mingling itself
with the articles of our faith, has occasioned no small
difficulties to Christians. For example, about the
Resurrection, how many scruples and objections have
been raised by Socinians and others? But do not the
most plausible of them depend on the suppositon that
a body is denominated the *same,* with regard not to the
form or that which is perceived by sense, but the material substance, which remains the same under several
forms? Take away this *material substance,* about the
identity whereof all the dispute is, and mean by *body*
what every plain ordinary person means by that word,
to wit, that which is immediately seen and felt, which
is only a combination of sensible qualities or ideas, and

then their most unanswerable objections come to nothing.

96. Matter being once expelled out of nature drags with it so many sceptical and impious notions, such an incredible number of disputes and puzzling questions, which have been thorns in the sides of divines as well as philosophers, and made so much fruitless work for mankind, that if the arguments we have produced against it are not found equal to demonstration (as to me they evidently seem), yet I am sure all friends to knowledge, peace, and religion have reason to wish they were.

97. Beside the external existence of the objects of perception, another great source of errors and difficulties with regard to ideal knowledge is the doctrine of *abstract ideas,* such as it hath been set forth in the Introduction. The plainest things in the world, those we are most intimately acquainted with and perfectly know, when they are considered in an abstract way, appear strangely difficult and incomprehensible.. Time, place, and motion, taken in particular or concrete, are what everybody knows, but, having passed through the hands of a metaphysician, they become too abstract and fine to be apprehended by men of ordinary sense. Bid your servant meet you at such a *time* in such a *place,* and he shall never stay to deliberate on the meaning of those words; in conceiving that particular time and place, or the motion by which he is to get thither, he finds not the least difficulty. But if *time* be taken exclusive of all those particular actions and ideas that diversify the day, merely for the continuation of existence or duration in abstract, then it will perhaps gravel even a philosopher to comprehend it.

98. For my own part, whenever I attempt to frame a simple idea of *time,* abstracted from the succession of ideas in my mind, which flows uniformly and is participated by all beings, I am lost and embrangled in inextricable difficulties. I have no notion of it at all, only I hear others say it is infinitely divisible, and speak of it in such a manner as leads me to entertain odd thoughts of my existence; since that doctrine lays one under an absolute necessity of thinking, either that he passes away innumerable ages without a thought, or else that he is annihilated every moment of his life, both which seem equally absurd. Time therefore being nothing, abstracted from the sucession of ideas in our minds, it follows that the duration of any finite spirit must be estimated by the number of ideas or actions succeeding each other in that same spirit or mind. Hence, it is a plain consequence that the soul always thinks; and in truth whoever shall go about to divide in his thoughts, or abstract the *existence* of a spirit from its *cogitation,* will, I believe, find it no easy task.

99. So likewise when we attempt to abtract extension and motion from all other qualities, and consider them by themselves, we presently lose sight of them, and run into great extravagances. [Hence spring those odd paradoxes, that the "fire is not hot," nor "the wall white," &c., or that heat and colour are in the objects nothing but figure and motion.]* All which depend on a twofold abstraction; first, it is supposed that extension, for example, may be abstracted from all other sensible qualities; and secondly, that the entity of extension may be abstracted from its being perceived. But, whoever shall reflect, and take care to

---

*Omitted in **second edition.**

understand what he says, will, if I mistake not, acknowledge that all sensible qualities are alike *sensations* and alike *real;* that where the extension is, there is the colour, too, *i. e.,* in his mind, and that their archetypes can exist only in some other *mind;* and that the objects of sense are nothing but those sensations combined, blended, or (if one may so speak) concreted together; none of all which can be supposed to exist unperceived. [And that consequently the wall is as truly white as it is extended, and in the same sense.]*

100. What it is for a man to be happy, or an object good, every one may think he knows. But to frame an abstract idea of happiness, prescinded from all particular pleasure, or of goodness from everything that is good, this is what few can pretend to. So likewise a man may be just and virtuous without having precise ideas of justice and virtue. The opinion that those and the like words stand for general notions, abstracted from all particular persons and actions, seems to have rendered morality very difficult, and the study thereof of small use to mankind. And in effect [one may make a great progress in school-ethics without ever being the wiser or better man for it, or knowing how to behave himself in the affairs of life more to the advantage of himself or his neighbours than he did before. This hint may suffice to let any one see]† the doctrine of *abstraction* has not a little contributed towards spoiling the most useful parts of knowledge.

101. The two great provinces of speculative science conversant about ideas received from sense, are Natu-

---

*The bracketed words were omitted in the second edition.
†Omitted in the second edition.

ral Philosophy and Mathematics; with regard to each
of these I shall make some observations. And first I
shall say somewhat of Natural Philosophy. On this
subject it is that the sceptics triumph. All that stock
of arguments they produce to depreciate our faculties
and make mankind appear ignorant and low, are
drawn principally from this head, namely, that we are
under an invincible blindness as to the *true* and *real*
nature of things. This they exaggerate, and love to
enlarge on. We are miserably bantered, say they, by
our senses, and amused only with the outside and show
of things. The real essence, the internal qualities and
constitution of every the meanest object, is hid from
our view; something there is in every drop of water,
every grain of sand, which it is beyond the power of
human understanding to fathom or comprehend. But,
it is evident from what has been shewn that all this
complaint is groundless, and that we are influenced by
false principles to that degree as to mistrust our senses,
and think we know nothing of those things which we
perfectly comprehend.

102. One great inducement to our pronouncing ourselves ignorant of the nature of things is the current
opinion that everything includes within itself the cause
of its properties; or that there is in each object an
inward essence which is the source whence its discernible qualities flow, and whereon they depend.
Some have pretended to account for appearances by
occult qualities, but of late they are mostly resolved
into mechanical causes, to wit, the figure, motion,
weight, and suchlike qualities, of insensible particles;
whereas, in truth, there is no other agent or efficient
cause than *spirit*, it being evident that motion, as well
as all other *ideas*, is perfectly inert. See sect. 25.

Hence, to endeavour to explain the production of colours or sounds, by figure, motion, magnitude, and the like, must needs be labour in vain. And accordingly we see the attempts of that kind are not at all satisfactory. Which may be said in general of those instances wherein one idea or quality is assigned for the cause of another. I need not say how many hypotheses and speculations are left out, and how much the study of nature is abridged by this doctrine.

103. The great mechanical principle now in vogue is *attraction*. That a stone falls to the earth, or the sea swells towards the moon, may to some appear sufficiently explained thereby. But how are we enlightened by being told this is done by attraction? Is it that that word signifies the manner of the tendency, and that it is by the mutual drawing of bodies instead of their being impelled or protruded towards each other? But, nothing is determined of the manner or action, and it may as truly (for aught we know) be termed "impulse," or "protrusion," as "attraction." Again, the parts of steel we see cohere firmly together, and this also is accounted for by attraction; but, in this as in the other instances, I do not perceive that anything is signified besides the effect itself; for as to the manner of the action whereby it is produced, or the cause which produces it, these are not so much as aimed at.

104. Indeed, if we take a view of the several phenomena, and compare them together, we may observe some likeness and conformity between them. For example, in the falling of a stone to the ground, in the rising of the sea towards the moon, in cohesion, crystallization, etc., there is something alike, namely, an union or mutual approach of bodies. So that any one

of these or the like phenomena may not seem strange or surprising to a man who has nicely observed and compared the effects of nature. For that only is thought so which is uncommon, or a thing by itself, and out of the ordinary course of our observation. That bodies should tend towards the centre of the earth is not thought strange, because it is what we perceive every moment of our lives. But, that they should have a like gravitation towards the centre of the moon may seem odd and unaccountable to most men, because it is discerned only in the tides. But a philosopher, whose thoughts take in a larger compass of nature, having observed a certain similitude of appearances, as well in the heavens as the earth, that argue innumerable bodies to have a mutual tendency towards each other, which he denotes by the general name "attraction," whatever can be reduced to that he thinks justly accounted for. Thus he explains the tides by the attraction of the terraqueous globe towards the moon, which to him does not appear odd or anomalous, but only a particular example of a general rule or law of nature.

105. If therefore we consider the difference there is betwixt natural philosophers and other men, with regard to their knowledge of the phenomena, we shall find it consists not in an exacter knowledge of the efficient cause that produces them—for that can be no other than the *will of a spirit*—but only in a greater largeness of comprehension, whereby analogies, harmonies, and agreements are discovered in the works of nature, and the particular effects explained, that is, reduced to general rules, see sect. 62, which rules, grounded on the analogy and uniformness observed in the production of natural effects, are most agreeable

and sought after by the mind; for that they extend our prospect beyond what is present and near to us, and enable us to make very probable conjectures touching things that may have happened at very great distances of time and place, as well as to predict things to come; which sort of endeavour towards omniscience is much affected by the mind.

106. But we should proceed warily in such things, for we are apt to lay too great stress on analogies, and, to the prejudice of truth, humour that eagerness of the mind whereby it is carried to extend its knowledge into general theorems. For example, in the business of gravitation or mutual attraction, because it appears in many instances, some are straightway for pronouncing it *universal;* and that to attract and be attracted by every other body is an essential quality inherent in all bodies whatsoever. Whereas it is evident the fixed stars have no such tendency towards each other; and, so far is that gravitation from being *essential* to bodies that in some instances a quite contrary principle seems to shew itself; as in the perpendicular growth of plants, and the elasticity of the air. There is nothing necessary or essential in the case, but it depends entirely on the will of the Governing Spirit, who causes certain bodies to cleave together or tend towards each other according to various laws, whilst He keeps others at a fixed distance; and to some He gives a quite contrary tendency to fly asunder just as He sees convenient.

107. After what has been premised, I think we may lay down the following conclusions. First, it is plain philosophers amuse themselves in vain, when they inquire for any natural efficient cause, distinct from a *mind* or *spirit.* Secondly, considering the whole crea-

tion is the workmanship of a *wise and good Agent,* it should seem to become philosophers to employ their thoughts (contrary to what some hold) about the final causes of things; [for, besides that this would prove a very pleasing entertainment to the mind, it might be of great advantage, in that it not only discovers to us the attributes of the Creator, but may also direct us in several instances to the proper uses and applications of things;]* and I confess I see no reason why pointing out the various ends to which natural things are adapted, and for which they were originally with unspeakable wisdom contrived, should not be thought one good way of accounting for them, and altogether worthy a philosopher. Thirdly, from what has been premised no reason can be drawn why the history of nature should not still be studied, and observations and experiments made, which, that they are of use to mankind, and enable us to draw any general conclusions, is not the result of any immutable habitudes or relations between things themselves, but only of God's goodness and kindness to men in the administration of the world. See sect. 30 and 31. Fourthly, by a diligent observation of the phenomena within our view, we may discover the general laws of nature, and from them deduce the other phenomena; I do not say *demonstrate,* for all deductions of that kind depend on a supposition that the Author of nature always operates uniformly, and in a constant observance of those rules we take for principles: which we cannot evidently know.

108. [It appears from sect. 66, &c., that the steady consistent methods of nature may not unfitly be styled the Language of its Author, whereby He discovers

---

*Omitted in second edition.

His attributes to our view and directs us how to act for the convenience and felicity of life. And to me]* those men who frame general rules from the phenomena and afterwards derive the phenomena from those rules, seem to consider signs rather than causes. A man may well understand natural signs without knowing their analogy, or being able to say by what rule a thing is so or so. And, as it is very possible to write improperly, through too strict an observance of general grammar rules; so, in arguing from general laws of nature, it is not impossible we may extend the analogy too far, and by that means run into mistakes.

109. As in reading other books a wise man will choose to fix his thoughts on the sense and apply it to use, rather than lay them out in grammatical remarks on the language; so, in perusing the volume of nature, it seems beneath the dignity of the mind to affect an exactness in reducing each particular phenomenon to general rules, or shewing how it follows from them. We should propose to ourselves nobler views, namely, to recreate and exalt the mind with a prospect of the beauty, order, extent, and variety of natural things: hence, by proper inferences, to enlarge our notions of the grandeur, wisdom, and beneficence of the Creator; and lastly, to make the several parts of the creation, so far as in us lies, subservient to the ends they were designed for, God's glory, and the sustentation and comfort of ourselves and fellow-creatures.

---

* The bracketed words were omitted in the second edition.

110.* The best key for the aforesaid analogy or natural Science will be easily acknowledged to be a certain celebrated Treatise of *Mechanics.* In the entrance of which justly admired treatise, Time, Space, and Motion are distinguished into *absolute* and *relative, true* and *apparent, mathematical* and *vulgar;* which distinction, as it is at large explained by the author, does suppose these quantities to have an existence without the mind; and that they are ordinarily conceived with relation to sensible things, to which nevertheless in their own nature they bear no relation at all.

111. As for *Time,* as it is there taken in an absolute or abstracted sense, for the duration or perseverance of the existence of things, I have nothing more to add concerning it after what has been already said on that subject. Sect. 97 and 98. For the rest, this celebrated author holds there is an *absolute Space,* which, being unperceivable to sense, remains in itself similar and immovable; and relative space to be the measure thereof, which, being movable and defined by its situation in respect of sensible bodies, is vulgarly taken for immovable space. *Place* he defines to be that part of space which is occupied by any body; and according

---

* Section 110 in the first edition began as follows: "The best grammar of the kind we are speaking of will be easily acknowledged to be a treatise of *Mechanics,* demonstrated and applied to nature by a philosopher of a neighboring nation whom all the world admire. I shall not take upon me to make remarks on the performance of that extraordinary person: only some things he has advanced so directly opposite to the doctrine we have hitherto laid down, that we should be wanting in the regard due to the authority of so great a man did we not take some notice of them. In the entrance," &c. The first edition appeared in Ireland; hence Newton is spoken of as belonging to a "neighboring nation."

as the space is absolute or relative so also is the place. *Absolute Motion* is said to be the translation of a body from absolute place to absolute place, as relative motion is from one relative place to another. And, because the parts of absolute space do not fall under our senses, instead of them we are obliged to use their sensible measures, and so define both place and motion with respect to bodies which we regard as immovable. But, it is said in philosophical matters we must abstract from our senses, since it may be that none of those bodies which seem to be quiescent are truly so, and the same thing which is moved relatively may be really at rest; as likewise one and the same body may be in relative rest and motion, or even moved with contrary relative motions at the same time, according as its place is variously defined. All which ambiguity is to be found in the apparent motions, but not at all in the true or absolute, which should therefore be alone regarded in philosophy. And the true as we are told are distinguished from apparent or relative motions by the following properties.—First, in true or absolute motion all parts which preserve the same position with respect of the whole, partake of the motions of the whole. Secondly, the place being moved, that which is placed therein is also moved; so that a body moving in a place which is in motion doth participate the motion of its place. Thirdly, true motion is never generated, or changed otherwise than by force impressed on the body itself. Fourthly, true motion is always changed by force impressed on the body moved. Fifthly, in circular motion barely relative there is no centrifugal force, which, nevertheless, in that which is true or absolute, is proportional to the quantity of motion.

112. But, notwithstanding what has been said, I must confess it does not appear to me that there can be any motion other than *relative;* so that to conceive motion there must be at least conceived two bodies, whereof the distance or position in regard to each other is varied. Hence, if there was one only body in being it could not possibly be moved. This seems evident, in that the idea I have of motion doth necessarily include relation.*

113. But, though in every motion it be necessary to conceive more bodies than one, yet it may be that one only is moved, namely, that on which the force causing the change in the distance or situation of the bodies, is impressed. For, however some may define relative motion, so as to term that body *moved* which changes its distance from some other body,† whether the force or action causing that change were impressed on it or no, yet as relative motion is that which is perceived by sense, and regarded in the ordinary affairs of life, it should seem that every man of common sense knows what it is as well as the best philosopher. Now, I ask any one whether, in his sense of motion as he walks along the streets, the stones he passes over may be said to *move,* because they change distance with his feet? To me it appears that though motion includes a relation of one thing to another, yet it is not necessary that each term of the relation be denominated from it. As a man may think of somewhat which

---

* In the first edition this section ended with the following sentence: "Whether others can conceive it otherwise, a little attention may satisfy them."

† In the first edition we had the following: "whether the force causing that change were impressed on it or no, yet I cannot assent to this; for, since we are told relative motion," &c.

does not think, so a body may be moved to or from another body which is not therefore itself in motion. [I mean relative motion, for other I am not able to conceive.]*

114. As the place happens to be variously defined, the motion which is related to it varies. A man in a ship may be said to be quiescent with relation to the sides of the vessel, and yet move with relation to the land. Or he may move eastward in respect of the one, and westward in respect of the other. In the common affairs of life men never go beyond the earth to define the place of any body; and what is quiescent in respect of that is accounted *absolutely* to be so. But philosophers, who have a greater extent of thought, and juster notions of the system of things, discover even the earth itself to be moved. In order therefore to fix their notions they seem to conceive the corporeal world as finite, and the utmost unmoved walls or shell thereof to be the place whereby they estimate true motions. If we sound our own conceptions, I believe we may find all the absolute motion we can frame an idea of to be at bottom no other than relative motion thus defined. For, as hath been already observed, absolute motion, exclusive of all external relation, is incomprehensible; and to this kind of relative motion all the above-mentioned properties, causes, and effects ascribed to absolute motion will, if I mistake not, be found to agree. As to what is said of the centrifugal force, that it does not at all belong to circular relative motion, I do not see how this follows from the experiment which is brought to prove it. See *Philosophiae Naturalis Principia Mathematica, in Schol. Def.*

---

*Omitted from second edition.

VIII. For the water in the vessel at that time wherein it is said to have the greatest relative circular motion, hath, I think, no motion at all; as is plain from the foregoing section.

115. For, to denominate a body *moved* it is requisite, first, that it change its distance or situation with regard to some other body; and secondly, that the force occasioning that change be applied to it. If either of these be wanting, I do not think that, agreeably to the sense of mankind, or the propriety of language, a body can be said to be in motion. I grant indeed that it is possible for us to think a body which we see change its distance from some other to be moved, though it have no force applied to it (in which sense there may be apparent motion), but then it is because the force causing the change of distance is imagined by us to be applied or impressed on that body thought to move; which indeed shews we are capable of mistaking a thing to be in motion which is not, and that is all,* [which is not, but does not prove that, in the common acceptation of motion, a body is moved merely because it changes distance from another; since as soon as we are undeceived, and find that the moving force was not communicated to it, we no longer hold it to be moved. So, on the other hand, when only one body (the parts whereof preserve a given position between themselves) is imagined to exist, some there are who think that it can be moved all manner of ways, though without any change of distance or situation to any other bodies; which we should not deny if they meant only that it might have an impressed force, which, upon the bare creation of

---

*In the first edition the phrase "and that is all" was omitted, and the paragraph closed with the sentences in brackets.

other bodies, would produce a motion of some certain quantity and determination. But that an actual motion (distinct from the impressed force or power productive of change of place in case there were bodies present whereby to define it) can exist in such a single body, I must confess I am not able to comprehend].

116. From what has been said it follows that the philosophic consideration of motion does not imply the being of an *absolute Space,* distinct from that which is perceived by sense and related bodies; which that it cannot exist without the mind is clear upon the same principles that demonstrate the like of all other objects of sense. And perhaps, if we enquire narrowly, we shall find we cannot even frame an idea of *pure Space* exclusive of all body. This I must confess seems impossible, as being a most abstract idea. When I excite a motion in some part of my body, if it be free or without resistance, I say there is *Space;* but if I find a resistance, then I say there is *Body;* and in proportion as the resistance to motion is lesser or greater, I say the space is more or less *pure.* So that when I speak of pure or empty space, it is not to be supposed that the word "space" stands for an idea distinct from or conceivable without body and motion—though indeed we are apt to think every noun substantive stands for a distinct idea that may be separated from all others; which has occasioned infinite mistakes. When, therefore, supposing all the world to be annihilated besides my own body, I say there still remains *pure Space,* thereby nothing else is meant but only that I conceive it possible for the limbs of my body to be moved on all sides without the least resistance, but if that, too, were annihilated then there could be no motion, and consequently no Space. Some, per-

haps, may think the sense of seeing doth furnish them with the idea of pure space; but it is plain from what we have elsewhere shewn, that the ideas of space and distance are not obtained by that sense. See the Essay concerning Vision.

117. What is here laid down seems to put an end to all those disputes and difficulties that have sprung up amongst the learned concerning the nature of *pure Space*. But the chief advantage arising from it is that we are freed from that dangerous dilemma, to which several who have employed their thoughts on that subject imagine themselves reduced, to wit, of thinking either that Real Space is God, or else that there is something beside God which is eternal, uncreated, infinite, indivisible, immutable. Both which may justly be thought pernicious and absurd notions. It is certain that not a few divines, as well as philosophers of great note, have, from the difficulty they found in conceiving either limits or annihilation of space, concluded it must be divine. And some of late have set themselves particularly to shew the incommunicable attributes of God agree to it. Which doctrine, how unworthy soever it may seem of the Divine Nature, yet I do not see how we can get clear of it, so long as we adhere to the received opinions.

118. Hitherto of Natural Philosophy: we come now to make some inquiry concerning that other great branch of speculative knowledge, to wit, Mathematics. These, how celebrated soever they may be for their clearness and certainty of demonstration, which is hardly anywhere else to be found, cannot nevertheless be supposed altogether free from mistakes, if in their principles there lurks some secret error which is com-

mon to the professors of those sciences with the rest of mankind. Mathematicians, though they deduce their theorems from a great height of evidence, yet their first principles are limited by the consideration of quantity: and they do not ascend into any inquiry concerning those transcendental maxims which influence all the particular sciences, each part whereof, Mathematics not excepted, does consequently participate of the errors involved in them. That the principles laid down by mathematicians are true, and their way of deduction from those principles clear and incontestible, we do not deny; but, we hold there may be certain erroneous maxims of greater extent than the object of Mathematics, and for that reason not expressly mentioned, though tacitly supposed throughout the whole progress of that science; and that the ill effects of those secret unexamined errors are diffused through all the branches thereof. To be plain, we suspect the mathematicians are as well as other men concerned in the errors arising from the doctrine of abstract general ideas, and the existence of objects without the mind.

119. Arithmetic has been thought to have for its object abstract ideas of *Number;* of which to understand the properties and mutual habitudes, is supposed no mean part of speculative knowledge. The opinion of the pure and intellectual nature of numbers in abstract has made them in esteem with those philosophers who seem to have affected an uncommon fineness and elevation of thought. It hath set a price on the most trifling numerical speculations which in practice are of no use, but serve only for amusement; and hath therefore so far infected the minds of some, that they have dreamed of mighty mysteries involved

in numbers, and attempted the explication of natural things by them. But, if we inquire into our own thoughts, and consider what has been premised, we may perhaps entertain a low opinion of those high flights and abstractions, and look on all inquiries, about numbers only as so many *difficiles nugae*, so far as they are not subservient to practice, and promote the benefit of life.

120. Unity in abstract we have before considered in sect. 13, from which and what has been said in the Introduction, it plainly follows there is not any such idea. But, number being defined a "collection of units," we may conclude that, if there be no such thing as unity or unit in abstract, there are no ideas of number in abstract denoted by the numeral names and figures. The theories therefore in Arithmetic, if they are abstracted from the names and figures, as likewise from all use and practice, as well as from the particular things numbered, can be supposed to have nothing at all for their object; hence we may see how entirely the science of numbers is subordinate to practice, and how jejune and trifling it becomes when considered as a matter of mere speculation.

121. However, since there may be some who, deluded by the specious show of discovering abstracted verities, waste their time in arithmetical theorems and problems which have not any use, it will not be amiss if we more fully consider and expose the vanity of that pretence; and this will plainly appear by taking a view of Arithmetic in its infancy, and observing what it was that originally put men on the study of that science, and to what scope they directed it. It is natural to think that at first, men, for ease of memory and help of computation, made use of counters,

or in writing of single strokes, points, or the like, each whereof was made to signify an unit, *i. e.,* some one thing of whatever kind they had occasion to reckon. Afterwards they found out the more compendious ways of making one character stand in place of several strokes or points. And, lastly, the notation of the Arabians or Indians came into use, wherein, by the repetition of a few characters or figures, and varying the signification of each figure according to the place it obtains, all numbers may be most aptly expressed; which seems to have been done in imitation of language, so that an exact analogy is observed betwixt the notation by figures and names, the nine simple figures answering the nine first numeral names and places in the former, corresponding to denominations in the latter. And agreeably to those conditions of the simple and local value of figures, were contrived methods of finding, from the given figures or marks of the parts, what figures and how placed are proper to denote the whole, or *vice versa.* And having found the sought figures, the same rule or analogy being observed throughout, it is easy to read them into words; and so the number becomes perfectly known. For then the number of any particular things is said to be known, when we know the name or figures (with their due arrangement) that according to the standing analogy belong to them. For, these signs being known, we can by the operations of arithmetic know the signs of any part of the particular sums signified by them; and, thus computing in signs (because of the connexion established betwixt them and the distinct multitudes of things whereof one is taken for an unit), we may be able rightly to sum up, divide, and proportion the things themselves that we intend to number.

122. In Arithmetic, therefore, we regard not the *things,* but the *signs,* which nevertheless are not regarded for their own sake, but because they direct us how to act with relation to things, and dispose rightly of them. Now, agreeably to what we have before observed of words in general (sect. 19, Introd.) it happens here likewise that abstract ideas are thought to be signified by numeral names or characters, while they do not suggest ideas of particular things to our minds. I shall not at present enter into a more particular dissertation on this subject, but only observe that it is evident from what has been said, those things which pass for abstract truths and theorems concerning numbers, are in reality conversant about no object distinct from particular numeral things, except only names and characters, which originally came to be considered on no other account but their being signs, or capable to represent aptly whatever particular things men had need to compute. Whence it follows that to study them for their own sake would be just as wise, and to as good purpose as if a man, neglecting the true use or original intention and subserviency of language, should spend his time in impertinent criticisms upon words, or reasonings and controversies purely verbal.

123. From numbers we proceed to speak of *Extension,* which, considered as relative,* is the object of Geometry. The *infinite* divisibility of *finite* extension, though it is not expressly laid down either as an axiom or theorem in the elements of that science, yet is throughout the same everywhere supposed and thought

---

*The words "considered as relative" were added to the last edition.

to have so inseparable and essential a connexion with the principles and demonstrations in Geometry, that mathematicians never admit it into doubt, or make the least question of it. And, as this notion is the source from whence do spring all those amusing geometrical paradoxes which have such a direct repugnancy to the plain common sense of mankind, and are admitted with so much reluctance into a mind not yet debauched by learning; so it is the principal occasion of all that nice and extreme subtilty which renders the study of Mathematics so difficult and tedious. Hence, if we can make it appear that no finite extension contains innumerable parts, or is infinitely divisible, it follows that we shall at once clear the science of Geometry from a great number of difficulties and contradictions which have ever been esteemed a reproach to human reason, and withal make the attainment thereof a business of much less time and pains than it hitherto has been.

124. Every particular finite extension which may possibly be the object of our thought is an *idea* existing only in the mind, and consequently each part thereof must be perceived. If, therefore, I cannot perceive innumerable parts in any finite extension that I consider, it is certain they are not contained in it; but, it is evident that I cannot distinguish innumerable parts in any particular line, surface, or solid, which I either perceive by sense, or figure to myself in my mind: wherefore I conclude they are not contained in it. Nothing can be plainer to me than that the extensions I have in view are no other than my own ideas; and it is no less plain that I cannot resolve any one of my ideas into an infinite number of other ideas, that is, that they are not infinitely divisible. If by

finite extension be meant something distinct from a finite idea, I declare I do not know what that is, and so cannot affirm or deny anything of it. But if the terms "extension," "parts," &c., are taken in any sense conceivable, that is, for ideas, then to say a finite quantity or extension consists of parts infinite in number is so manifest a contradiction, that every one at first sight acknowledges it to be so; and it is impossible it should ever gain the assent of any reasonable creature who is not brought to it by gentle and slow degrees, as a converted Gentile to the belief of transubstantiation. Ancient and rooted prejudices do often pass into principles; and those propositions which once obtain the force and credit of a *principle,* are not only themselves, but likewise whatever is deducible from them, thought privileged from all examination. And there is no absurdity so gross, which, by this means, the mind of man may not be prepared to swallow.

125. He whose understanding is possessed with the doctrine of abstract general ideas may be persuaded that (whatever be thought of the ideas of sense) extension in *abstract* is infinitely divisible. And one who thinks the objects of sense exist without the mind will perhaps in virtue thereof be brought to admit that a line but an inch long may contain innumerable parts—really existing, though too small to be discerned. These errors are grafted as well in the minds of geometricians as of other men, and have a like influence on their reasonings; and it were no difficult thing to shew how the arguments from Geometry made use of to support the infinite divisibility of extension are bottomed on them. [But this, if it be thought necessary, we may hereafter find a proper place to treat

of in a particular manner.]*   At present we shall only observe in general whence it is the mathematicians are all so fond and tenacious of that doctrine.

126. It hath been observed in another place that the theorems and demonstrations in Geometry are conversant about universal ideas (sect. 15, Introd.) ; where it is explained in what sense this ought to be understood, to wit, the particular lines and figures included in the diagram are supposed to stand for innumerable others of different sizes ; or, in other words, the geometer considers them abstracting from their magnitude—which does not imply that he forms an abstract idea, but only that he cares not what the particular magnitude is, whether great or small, but looks on that as a thing different to the demonstration.   Hence it follows that a line in the scheme but an inch long must be spoken of as though it contained ten thousand parts, since it is regarded not in itself, but as it is universal; and it is universal only in its signification, whereby it represents innumerable lines greater than itself, in which may be distinguished ten thousand parts or more, though there may not be above an inch in it. After this manner, the properties of the lines signified are (by a very usual figure) transferred to the sign, and thence, through mistake, thought to appertain to it considered in its own nature.

127. Because there is no number of parts so great but it is possible there may be a line containing more, the inch-line is said to contain parts more than any assignable number ; which is true, not of the inch taken absolutely, but only for the things signified by it.   But men, not retaining that distinction in their thoughts, slide into a belief that the small particular line described

---

*Omitted in second edition.

on paper contains in itself parts innumerable. There is no such thing as the ten thousandth part of an inch; but there is of a mile or diameter of the earth, which may be signified by that inch. When therefore I delineate a triangle on paper, and take one side not above an inch, for example, in length to be the radius, this I consider as divided into 10,000 or 100,000 parts or more; for, though the ten thousandth part of that line considered in itself is nothing at all, and consequently may be neglected without an error or inconveniency, yet these described lines, being only marks standing for greater quantities, whereof it may be the ten thousandth part is very considerable, it follows that, to prevent notable errors in practice, the radius must be taken of 10,000 parts or more.

128. From what has been said the reason is plain why, to the end any theorem become universal in its use, it is necessary we speak of the lines described on paper as though they contained parts which really they do not. In doing of which, if we examine the matter thoroughly, we shall perhaps discover that we cannot conceive an inch itself as consisting of, or being divisible into, a thousand parts, but only some other line which is far greater than an inch, and represented by it; and that when we say a line is infinitely divisible, we must mean* a line which is infinitely great. What we have here observed seems to be the chief cause why, to suppose the infinite divisibility of finite extension has been thought necessary in geometry.

129. The several absurdities and contradictions which flowed from this false principle might, one

---

*In the first edition: "we mean (if we mean anything) a line which is," &c.

would think, have been esteemed so many demonstrations against it. But, by I know not what logic, it is held that proofs *a posteriori* are not to be admitted against propositions relating to infinity, as though it were not impossible even for an infinite mind to reconcile contradictions; or as if anything absurd and repugnant could have a necessary connexion with truth or flow from it. But, whoever considers the weakness of this pretence will think it was contrived on purpose to humour the laziness of the mind which had rather acquiesce in an indolent scepticism than be at the pains to go through with a severe examination of those principles it has ever embraced for true.

130. Of late the speculations about Infinites have run so high, and grown to such strange notions, as have occasioned no small scruples and disputes among the geometers of the present age. Some there are of great note who, not content with holding that finite lines may be divided into an infinite number of parts, do yet farther maintain that each of those infinitesimals is itself subdivisible into an infinity of other parts or infinitesimals of a second order, and so on *ad infinitum*. These, I say, assert there are infinitesimals of infinitesimals of infinitesimals, &c., without ever coming to an end: so that according to them an inch does not barely contain an infinite number of parts, but an infinity of an infinity of an infinity *ad infinitum* of parts. Others there be who hold all orders of infinitesimals below the first to be nothing at all; thinking it with good reason absurd to imagine there is any positive quantity or part of extension which, though multiplied infinitely, can never equal the smallest given extension. And yet on the other hand it seems no less absurd to think the square, cube or other power of a positive real

root, should itself be nothing at all; which they who hold infinitesimals of the first order, denying all of the subsequent orders, are obliged to maintain.

131. Have we not therefore reason to conclude they are *both* in the wrong, and that there is in effect no such thing as parts infinitely small, or an infinite number of parts contained in any finite quantity? But you will say that if this doctrine obtains it will follow the very foundations of Geometry are destroyed, and those great men who have raised that science to so astonishing a height, have been all the while building a castle in the air. To this it may be replied that whatever is useful in geometry, and promotes the benefit of human life, does still remain firm and unshaken on our principles; that science considered as practical will rather receive advantage than any prejudice from what has been said. But to set this in a due light [and show how lines and figures may be measured, and their properties investigated, without supposing finite extension to be infinitely divisible]* may be the proper business of another place. For the rest, though it should follow that some of the more intricate and subtle parts of Speculative Mathematics may be pared off without any prejudice to truth, yet I do not see what damage will be thence derived to mankind. On the contrary, I think it were highly to be wished that men of great abilities and obstinate application would draw off their thoughts from those amusements, and employ them in the study of such things as lie nearer the concerns of life, or have a more direct influence on the manners.

132. If it be said that several theorems undoubtedly true are discovered by methods in which infinitesimals

---

*Omitted in second edition.

are made use of, which could never have been if their existence included a contradiction in it; I answer that upon a thorough examination it will not be found that in any instance it is necessary to make use of or conceive infinitesimal parts of finite lines, or even quantities less than the *minimum sensible;* nay, it will be evident this is never done, it being impossible.   [And, whatever mathematicians may think of fluxions, or the differential calculus and the like, a little reflexion will shew them that, in working by those methods, they do not conceive or imagine lines or surfaces less than what are perceivable to sense.   They may indeed call those little and almost insensible quantities infinitesimals, or infinitesimals of infinitesimals, if they please; but at bottom this is all, they being in truth finite; nor does the solution of problems require the supposing any other.   But this will be more clearly made out hereafter.]*

133. By what we have premised, it is plain that very numerous and important errors have taken their rise from those false Principles which were impugned in the foregoing parts of this treatise; and the opposites of those erroneous tenets at the same time appear to be most fruitful Principles, from whence do flow innumerable consequences highly advantageous to true philosophy, as well as to religion.   Particularly *Matter,* or *the absolute existence of corporeal objects,* hath been shewn to be that wherein the most avowed and pernicious enemies of all knowledge, whether human or divine, have ever placed their chief strength and confidence.   And surely, if by distinguishing the real exist-

---

*Bracketed sentences omitted in second edition.

ence of unthinking things from their being perceived. and allowing them a subsistance of their own out of the minds of spirits, no one thing is explained in nature, but on the contrary a great many inexplicable difficulties arise; if the supposition of Matter is barely precarious, as not being grounded on so much as one single reason; if its consequences cannot endure the light of examination and free inquiry, but screen themselves under the dark and general pretence of "infinites being incomprehensible;" if withal the removal of this *Matter* be not attended with the least evil consequence; if it be not even missed in the world, but everything as well, nay much easier conceived without it; if, lastly, both Sceptics and Atheists are for ever silenced upon supposing only spirits and ideas, and this scheme of things is perfectly agreeable both to Reason and Religion: methinks we may expect it should be admitted and firmly embraced, though it were proposed only as an *hypothesis,* and the existence of Matter had been allowed possible, which yet I think we have evidently demonstrated that it is not.

134. True it is that, in consequence of the foregoing principles, several disputes and speculations which are esteemed no mean parts of learning, are rejected as useless.* But, how great a prejudice soever against our notions this may give to those who have already been deeply engaged, and made large advances in studies of that nature, yet by others we hope it will not be thought any just ground of dislike to the principles and tenets herein laid down, that they abridge the labour of study, and make human sciences far more

---

*"Useless and in effect conversant about nothing at all," in first edition.

clear, compendious and attainable than they were before.

135. Having despatched what we intended to say
concerning the knowledge of IDEAS, the method we
proposed leads us in the next place to treat of SPIRITS
—with regard to which, perhaps, human knowledge is
not so deficient as is vulgarly imagined. The great
reason that is assigned for our being thought ignorant
of the nature of spirits is our not having an *idea* of it.
But, surely it ought not to be looked on as a defect in
a human understanding that it does not perceive the
idea of spirit, if it is manifestly impossible there should
be any such idea. And this if I mistake not has been
demonstrated in section 27; to which I shall here add
that a spirit has been shewn to be the only substance
or support wherein unthinking beings or ideas can
exist; but that this *substance* which supports or perceives ideas should itself be an idea or like an idea is
evidently absurd.

136. It will perhaps be said that we want a sense (as
some have imagined) proper to know substances withal,
which, if we had, we might know our own soul as we
do a triangle. To this I answer, that, in case we had a
new sense bestowed upon us, we could only receive
thereby some new sensations or ideas of sense. But I
believe nobody will say that what he means by the
terms *soul* and *substance* is only some particular sort
of idea or sensation. We may therefore infer that, all
things duly considered, it is not more reasonable to
think our faculties defective, in that they do not furnish
us with an idea of spirit or active thinking substance,
than it would be if we should blame them for not being able to comprehend a *round square*.

137. From the opinion that spirits are to be known after the manner of an idea or sensation have risen many absurd and heterodox tenets, and much scepticism about the nature of the soul. It is even probable that this opinion may have produced a doubt in some whether they had any soul at all distinct from their body, since upon inquiry they could not find they had an idea of it. That an *idea* which is inactive, and the existence whereof consists in being perceived, should be the image or likeness of an agent subsisting by itself, seems to need no other refutation than barely attending to what is meant by those words. But, perhaps you will say that though an idea cannot resemble a spirit in its thinking, acting, or subsisting by itself, yet it may in some other respects; and it is not necessary that an idea or image be in all respects like the original.

138. I answer, if it does not in those mentioned, it is impossible it should represent it in any other thing. Do but leave out the power of willing, thinking, and perceiving ideas, and there remains nothing else wherein the idea can be like a spirit. For, by the word *spirit* we mean only that which thinks, wills, and perceives; this, and this alone, constitutes the signification of that term. If therefore it is impossible that any degree of those powers should be represented in an idea, * it is evident there can be no idea of a spirit.

139. But it will be objected that, if there is no idea signified by the terms *soul, spirit, and substance,* they are wholly insignificant, or have no meaning in them. I answer, those words do mean or signify a real thing,

---

*In the first edition, for "idea" in both places in this sentence, we had "idea *or notion.*" Compare section 142.

which is neither an idea nor like an idea, but that which
perceives ideas, and wills, and reasons about them.
What I am myself, that which I denote by the term *I,*
is the same with what is meant by   *soul* or *spiritual
subtance.** If it be said that this is only quarreling at
a word, and that, since the immediately significations
of other names are by common consent called *ideas,* no
reason can be assigned why that which is signified by
the name *spirit* or *soul* may not partake in the same ap-
pellation.   I answer, all the unthinking objects of the
mind agree in that they are entirely passive, and their
existence consists only in being perceived; whereas a
soul or spirit is an active being, whose existence consists, not in being perceived, but in perceiving ideas and
thinking.   It is therefore necessary, in order to prevent equivocation and confounding natures perfectly
disagreeing and unlike, that we distinguish between
spirit and *idea.*   See sect. 27.

140. In a large sense, indeed, we may be said to have
an idea or rather a notion of *spirit;†* that is, we understand the meaning of the word, otherwise we could
not affirm or deny anything of it.   Moreover, as we
conceive the ideas that are in the minds of other spirits
by means of our own, which we suppose to be resemblances of them; so we know other spirits by means
of our own soul—which in that sense is the image or
idea of them; it having a like respect to other spirits
that blueness or heat by me perceived has to those
ideas perceived by another.

---

*In the first edition the following occurred at this point:
"But if I should say that *I* was nothing, or that *I* was an idea
or notion, nothing could be more evidently absurd than either
of these propositions."

†The words "or rather a notion" were inserted in the second
edition.   See section 142.

141. [The *natural immortality of the soul* is a necessary consequence of the foregoing doctrine. But before we attempt to prove this, it is fit that we explain the meaning of that tenet.]*. It must not be supposed that they who assert the natural immortality of the soul are of opinon that it is absolutely incapable of annihilation even by the infinite power of the Creator who first gave it being, but only that it is not liable to be broken or dissolved by the ordinary laws of nature or motion. They indeed who hold the soul of man to be only a thin vital flame, or system of animal spirits, make it perishing and corruptible as the body; since there is nothing more easily dissipated than such a being, which it is naturally impossible should survive the ruin of the tabernacle wherein it is enclosed. And this notion has been greedily embraced and cherished by the worst part of mankind, as the most effectual antidote against all impressions of virtue and religion. But it has been made evident that bodies, of what frame or texture soever, are barely passive ideas in the mind, which is more distant and heterogeneous from them than light is from darkness. We have shewn that the soul is indivisible, incorporeal, unextended, and it is consequently incorruptible. Nothing can be plainer than that the motions, changes, decays, and dissolutions which we hourly see befall natural bodies (and which is what we mean by the *course of nature*) cannot possibly affect an active, simple, uncompounded substance; such a being therefore is indissoluble by the force of nature; that is to say, "the soul of man is naturally immortal."

142. After what has been said, it is, I suppose, plain

---

*Omitted from second edition.

that our souls are not to be known in the same manner as senseless, inactive objects, or by way of *idea*.
Spirits and *ideas* are things so wholly different, that
when we say "they exist," "they are known," or the
like, these words must not be thought to signify anything common to both natures. There is nothing alike or
common in them: and to expect that by any multiplica-
tion or enlargement of our faculties we may be enabled
to know a spirit as we do a triangle, seems as absurd
as if we should hope to see a sound.   This is incul-
cated because I imagine it may be of moment towards
clearing several important questions, and preventing
some very dangerous errors concerning the nature of
the soul.   [We may not, I think, strictly be said to have
an *idea* of an active being, or of an action, although
we may be said to have a *notion* of them.   I have some
knowledge or notion of my mind, and its acts about
ideas, inasmuch as I know or understand what is meant
by these words.   What I know, that I have some notion
of. I will not say that the terms *idea* and *notion* may not
be used convertibly, if the world will have it so; but yet
it conduceth to clearness and propriety that we distinguish things very different by different names.   It
is also to be remarked that, all relations including an
act of the mind, we cannot so properly be said to have
an idea, but rather a notion of the relations and habitudes between things.   But if, in the modern way, the
word *idea* is extended to spirits, and relations, and acts,
this is, after all, an affair of verbal concern.]*

143. It will not be amiss to add, that the doctrine of
abstract ideas has had no small share in rendering
those sciences intricate and obscure which are particu-

---

*The sentences in brackets were inserted in the second
edition.

larly conversant about spiritual things. Men have imagined they could frame abstract notions of the powers and acts of the mind, and consider them prescinded as well from the mind or spirit itself, as from their respective objects and effects. Hence a great number of dark and ambiguous terms, presumed to stand for abstract notions, have been introduced into metaphysics and morality, and from these have grown infinite distractions and disputes amongst the learned.

144. But, nothing seems more to have contributed towards engaging men in controversies and mistakes with regard to the nature and operations of the mind, than the being used to speak of those things in terms borrowed from sensible ideas. For example, the will is termed the *motion* of the soul: this infuses a belief that the mind of man is as a ball in motion, impelled and determined by the objects of sense, as necessarily as that is by the stroke of a racket. Hence arise endless scruples and errors of dangerous consequence in morality. All which, I doubt not, may be cleared, and truth appear plain, uniform, and consistent, could but philosophers be prevailed on to retire into themselves, and attentively consider their own meaning.*

145. From what has been said, it is plain that we cannot know the existence of other spirits otherwise than by their operations, or the ideas by them excited in us. I perceive several motions, changes, and combinations of ideas, that inform me there are certain particular agents, like myself, which accompany them

---

*In the first edition the last part of this sentence and section reads: "could but philosophers be prevailed on to depart from some received prejudices and modes of speech, and retire into themselves, and attentively consider their own maning. But the difficulties arising on this head demand a more particular disquisition than suits with the design of this treatise."

and concur in their production. Hence, the knowledge
I have of other spirits is not immediate, as is the
knowledge of my ideas; but depending on the intervention of ideas, by me referred to agents or spirits
distinct from myself, as effects or concomitant signs.

146. But, though there be some things which convince us human agents are concerned in producing
them; yet it is evident to every one that those things
which are called the Works of Nature, that is, the far
greater part of the ideas or sensations perceived by us,
are not produced by, or dependent on, the wills of men.
There is therefore some other Spirit that causes them;
since it is repugnant that they should subsist by themselves. See sect. 29. But, if we attentively consider
the constant regularity, order, and concatenation of
natural things, the surprising magnificence, beauty,
and perfection of the larger, and the exquisite contrivance of the smaller parts of creation, together with
the exact harmony and correspondence of the whole,
but above all the never-enough-admired laws of pain
and pleasure, and the instincts or natural inclinations,
appetites, and passions of animals; I say if we consider all these things, and at the same time attend to
the meaning and import of the attributes One, Eternal,
Infinitely Wise, Good, and Perfect, we shall clearly
perceive that they belong to the aforesaid Spirit, "who
works all in all," and "by whom all things consist."

147. Hence, it is evident that God is known as certainly and immediately as any other mind or spirit
whatsoever distinct from ourselves. We may even
assert that the existence of God is far more evidently
perceived than the existence of men; because the effects of nature are infinitely more numerous and considerable than those ascribed to human agents. There

is not any one mark that denotes a man, or effect produced by him, which does not more strongly evince the being of that Spirit who is the Author of Nature. For, it is evident that in affecting other persons the will of man has no other object than barely the motion of the limbs of his body; but that such a motion should be attended by, or excite any idea in the mind of another, depends wholly on the will of the Creator. He alone it is who, "upholding all things by the word of His power," maintains that intercourse between spirits whereby they are able to perceive the existence of each other. And yet this pure and clear light which enlightens every one is itself invisible.*

148. It seems to be a general pretence of the unthinking herd that they cannot *see* God. Could we but see Him, say they, as we see a man, we should believe that He is, and believing obey His commands. But alas, we need only open our eyes to see the Sovereign Lord of all things, with a more full and clear view than we do any one of our fellow-creatures. Not that I imagine we see God (as some will have it) by a direct and immediate view; or see corporeal things, not by themselves, but by seeing that which represents them in the essence of God, which doctrine is, I must confess, to me incomprehensible. But I shall explain my meaning:—A human spirit or person is not perceived by sense, as not being an idea; when therefore we see the colour, size, figure, and motions of a man, we perceive only certain sensations or ideas excited in our own minds; and these being exhibited to our view in sundry distinct collections, serve to mark out unto us the existence of finite and created spirits like ourselves.

---

*"Invisible to the greatest part of mankind," in first edition.

Hence it is plain we do not see a man—if by *man* is meant that which lives, moves, perceives, and thinks as we do—but only such a certain collection of ideas as directs us to think there is a distinct principle of thought and motion, like to ourselves, accompanying and represented by it. And after the same manner we see God; all the difference is that, whereas some one finite and narrow assemblage of ideas denotes a particular human mind, whithersoever we direct our view, we do at all times and in all places perceive manifest tokens of the Divinity: everything we see, hear, feel, or anywise perceive by sense, being a sign or effect of the power of God; as is our perception of those very motions which are produced by men.

149. It is therefore plain that nothing can be more evident to any one that is capable of the least reflexion than the existence of God, or a Spirit who is intimately present to our minds, producing in them all that variety of ideas or sensations which continually affect us, on whom we have an absolute and entire dependence, in short "in whom we live, and move, and have our being." That the discovery of this great truth, which lies so near and obvious to the mind, should be attained to by the reason of so very few, is a sad instance of the stupidity and inattention of men, who, though they are surrounded with such clear manifestations of the Deity, are yet so little affected by them that they seem, as it were, blinded with excess of light.

150. But you will say, Hath Nature no share in the production of natural things, and must they be all ascribed to the immediate and sole operation of God? I answer, if by *Nature* is meant only the visible *series* of effects or sensations imprinted on our minds, according to certain fixed and general laws, then it is plain that

Nature, taken in this sense, cannot produce anything at all. But, if by *Nature* is meant some being distinct from God, as well as from the laws of nature, and things perceived by sense, I must confess that word is to me an empty sound without any intelligible meaning annexed to it. Nature, in this acceptation, is a vain chimera, introduced by those heathens who had not just notions of the omnipresence and infinite perfection of God. But, it is more unaccountable that it should be received among Christians, professing belief in the Holy Scriptures, which constantly ascribe those effects to the immediate hand of God that heathen philosophers are wont to impute to Nature. "The Lord He causeth the vapours to ascend; He maketh lightnings with rain; He bringeth forth the wind out of his treasures." Jerem. x. 13. "He turneth the shadow of death into the morning, and maketh the day dark with night." Amos v. 8. "He visiteth the earth, and maketh it soft with showers: He blesseth the springing thereof, and crowneth the year with His goodness; so that the pastures are clothed with flocks, and the valleys are covered over with corn." See Psalm lxv. But, notwithstanding that this is the constant language of Scripture, yet we have I know not what aversion from believing that God concerns Himself so nearly in our affairs. Fain would we suppose Him at a great distance off, and substitute some blind unthinking deputy in His stead, though (if we may believe Saint Paul) "He be not far from every one of us."

151. It will, I doubt not, be objected that the slow and gradual methods observed in the production of natural things do not seem to have for their cause the immediate hand of an Almighty Agent. Besides, monsters, untimely births, fruits blasted in the blossom,

rains falling in desert places, miseries incident to human life, and the like, are so many arguments that the whole frame of nature is not immediately actuated and superintended by a Spirit of infinite wisdom and goodness.   But the answer to this objection is in a good measure plain from sect. 62; it being visible that the aforesaid methods of nature are absolutely necessary, in order to working by the most simple and general rules, and after a steady and consistent manner; which argues both the wisdom and goodness of God. [For, it doth hence follow that the finger of God is not so conspicuous to the resolved and careless sinner, which gives him an opportunity to harden in his impiety and grow ripe for vengeance. (Vide sect. 57.)]* Such is the artificial contrivance of this mighty machine of nature that, whilst its motions and various phenomena strike on our senses, the hand which actuates the whole is itself unperceivable to men of flesh and blood. "Verily" (saith the prophet) "thou art a God that hidest thyself." Isaiah xlv. 15. But, though the Lord conceal Himself from the eyes of the sensual and lazy, who will not be at the least expense of thought, yet to an unbiased and attentive mind nothing can be more plainly legible than the intimate presence of an All-wise Spirit, who fashions, regulates, and sustains the whole system of beings. It is clear, from what we have elsewhere observed, that the operating according to general and stated laws is so necessary for our guidance in the affairs of life, and letting us into the secret of nature, that without it all reach and compass of thought, all human sagacity and design, could serve to no manner of purpose; it were even impossible there

---

*Omitted from second edition.

should be any such faculties or powers in the mind.
See sect. 31. Which one consideration abundantly out-
balances whatever particular inconveniences may
thence arise.

152. We should further consider that the very
blemishes and defects of nature are not without their
use, in that they make an agreeable sort of variety, and
augment the beauty of the rest of the creation, as shades
in a picture serve to set off the brighter and more enlightened parts. We would likewise do well to examine whether our taxing the waste of seeds and embryos,
and accidental destruction of plants and animals, before they come to full maturity, as an imprudence in the
Author of nature, be not the effect of prejudice con-
tracted by our familiarity with impotent and saving
mortals. In man indeed a thrifty management of those
things which he cannot procure without much pains
and industry may be esteemed wisdom. But, we must
not imagine that the inexplicably fine machine of an
animal or vegetable costs the great Creator any more
pains or trouble in its production than a pebble does;
nothing being more evident than that an Omnipotent
Spirit can indifferently produce everything by a mere
fiat or act of His will. Hence, it is plain that the splen-
did profusion of natural things should not be interpreted weakness or prodigality in the agent who produces them, but rather be looked on as an argument of
the riches of His power.

153. As for the mixture of pain or uneasiness which
is in the world, pursuant to the general laws of nature,
and the actions of finite, imperfect spirits, this, in the
state we are in at present, is indispensably necessary to
our well-being. But our prospects are too narrow. We
take, for instance, the idea of some one particular pain

into our thoughts, and account it *evil;* whereas, if we enlarge our view, so as to comprehend the various ends, connexions, and dependencies of things, on what occasions and in what proportions we are affected with pain and pleasure, the nature of human freedom, and the design with which we are put into the world; we shall be forced to acknowledge that those particular things which, considered in themselves, appear to be evil, have the nature of good, when considered as linked with the whole system of beings.

154. From what has been said, it will be manifest to any considering person, that it is merely for want of attention and comprehensiveness of mind that there are any favourers of Atheism or the Manichean Heresy to be found. Little and unreflecting souls may indeed burlesque the works of Providence the beauty and order whereof they have not capacity, or will not be at the pains, to comprehend; but those who are masters of any justness and extent of thought, and are withal used to reflect, can never sufficiently admire the divine traces of Wisdom and Goodness that shine throughout the Economy of Nature. But what truth is there which shineth so strongly on the mind that by an aversion of thought, a wilful shutting of the eyes, we may not escape seeing it [at least with a full and direct view]?* Is it therefore to be wondered at, if the generality of men, who are ever intent on business or pleasure, and little used to fix or open the eye of their mind, should not have all that conviction and evidence of the Being of God which might be expected in reasonable creatures?

155. We should rather wonder that men can be found so stupid as to neglect, than that neglecting they should

---

*Omitted from second edition.

be unconvinced of such an evident and momentous
truth. And yet it is to be feared that too many of parts
and leisure, who live in Christian countries, are, merely
through a supine and dreadful negligence, sunk into
Atheism.* Since it is downright impossible that a soul
pierced and enlightened with a thorough sense of the
omnipresence, holiness, and justice of that Almighty
Spirit should persist in a remorseless violation of His
laws. We ought, therefore, earnestly to meditate and
dwell on those important points; that so we may attain
conviction without all scruple "that the eyes of the
Lord are in every place beholding the evil and the good;
that He is with us and keepeth us in all places whither
we go, and giveth us bread to eat and raiment to put
on;" that He is present and conscious to our innermost
thoughts; and that we have a most absolute and immediate dependence on Him. A clear view of which great
truths cannot choose but fill our hearts with an awful
circumspection and holy fear, which is the strongest
incentive to *Virtue,* and the best guard against *Vice.*

156. For, after all, what deserves the first place in
our studies is the consideration of GOD and our DUTY;
which to promote, as it was the main drift and design
of my labours, so shall I esteem them altogether useless
and ineffectual if, by what I have said, I cannot inspire
my readers with a pious sense of the Presence of God;
and, having shewn the falseness or vanity of those
barren speculations which make the chief employment

---

*This paragraph read as follows in the first edition: "sunk
into a sort of Demy-Atheism. They cannot say there is not a
God, but neither are they convinced that there is. For what
else can it be but some lurking infidelity, some secret misgiv-
ings of mind with regard to the existence and attributes of
God, which permits sinners to grow and harden in impiety?
Since it is downright," &c.

of learned men, the better dispose them to reverence **and** embrace the salutary truths of the Gospel, which to know and to practice is the highest perfection of human nature.